Let Justice Roll Down

Let Justice Roll Down

*A Christian Aid/CAFOD Anthology for
Lent, Holy Week and Easter*

Compiled by
Geoffrey Duncan

CANTERBURY
PRESS
Norwich

© in this compilation Geoffrey Duncan 2003

First published in 2003 by the Canterbury Press Norwich
(a publishing imprint of Hymns Ancient & Modern Limited,
a registered charity)
St Mary's Works, St Mary's Plain,
Norwich, Norfolk, NR3 3BH

www.scm-canterburypress.co.uk

British Library Cataloguing in Publication data

A catalogue record for this book is available
from the British Library

ISBN 1-85311-555-X

Typeset by Regent Typesetting
Printed and bound by
Biddles Ltd, www.biddles.co.uk

Contents

Foreword

The liturgical traditions that Christians draw upon in celebrating Lent, Passiontide and Easter are not only among the oldest forms of Christian worship, they are also surely the richest. The suffering, death and resurrection of Jesus that inspired the development of liturgy, worship and ritual throughout the history of the church continue to inspire people today to produce reflections and prayers for their own time, that are born out of their own experiences.

This new anthology takes us from Shrove Tuesday to Easter Sunday. We begin by praying that we might 'fast from unkind thoughts' and end by asking that we might say with Thomas 'my Lord and my God'. The contributions take many different forms. Alongside a wide variety of prayers and reflections, there are liturgies of repentance for Ash Wednesday and dramatic representations of some of the events of Holy Week and Easter. The writers come from many countries, but one theme that emerges particularly from much of their work is a concern for healing and justice for people who find themselves suffering or marginalized in our world today.

Two previous anthologies, also compiled by Geoffrey Duncan, *Shine on, Star of Bethlehem* and *Harvest for the World*, have already been a notable success for the collaboration between Christian Aid and Canterbury Press. This third book, which completes the trilogy, is a three-way collaboration. CAFOD's participation has added a significant further dimension, with contributions from a distinctive Catholic tradition that combines spirituality with a deep longing for justice.

So we are led to reflect on the mystery of Christ's suffering and the wonder of his resurrection, but without losing sight of the very down-to-earth implications of those events for our lives today. As Paulo Freire puts it:

vii

Washing one's hands of the conflict
between the powerful and the powerless
means to side with the powerful,
not to be neutral.

Chris Bain　　　　　　　　　*Daleep Mukarji*
CAFOD Director　　　　　　*Director, Christian Aid*

Part One

Shrove Tuesday, Ash Wednesday and the Beginning of Lent

A Time for Reflection

'You desire truth in the inward being, therefore teach me wisdom in my secret heart.' (Psalm 51:6)

A True Saying

If we forget our merits
God will forget our sins

Source unknown

Shrove Tuesday

Stir in the flour with the eggs.
Pour in the milk.
Beat it all up, and make it suffer,
For Lent is coming,
Time of hardship,
For I am a sinner.

Caress the flour with the eggs.
Trickle in the milk.
Gently mix it all together,
For Lent is coming,
Time of growth,
For I am blessed.

Who are you, Lord?
God of judgement? God of Love?
Honey sweet or lemon sour?
Each pancake tells its tale.

Sarah Ingle
England

Not Only in Lent, Lord

Help me to fast from unkind thoughts,
from words much better left unsaid,
and judgements made from lack of love
hidden resentments may have fed.

3

Nourish me, Lord; with every breath
may I drink in your love and light,
to taste and know that growing peace
which brings a different appetite.

Cecily Taylor
England

The Ash Cross

Actions by Christian peacemakers during Lent at military sites, establishments and government buildings, contribute to the naming and uncovering of those things which perpetuate violence and injustice. Making the sign of the cross or writing the word 'Repent', with blessed ash and charcoal on a building may seem rather extreme. However, this kind of witness can create a space for Christians to express their full humanity, fears, anger, faith, hope – at a place where work to deny and destroy life is in progress. They are saying, for themselves and the Christian community who join them, 'What happens here is not the way of God.'

Pax Christi
Britain

Ash Wednesday Liturgy

In the Australian bush, fire often consumes the trees and grass leaving the landscape charred. Several days after the fire, shoots sprout from the grass roots as well as the stumps and branches and make a brilliant cover of green over the fire-blackened bark and earth.

We come to be united with the blackened earth as we receive the mark of ash on our skin. Just as new growth surely follows the fire so new things await us as we make this journey of repentance.

Because we have covered ourselves with pride and arrogance:
Cleanse and set us free.

Since we have been content with the empty and the superficial:
Fill us from the depths of love.

When we become trapped in old patterns and struggles:
Lift our eyes in hope.

Even though we are broken and far short of perfection:
Form us for loving service.

After our best efforts have met with rejection and discouragement:
Encourage us still to trust.

So we bring before God all that is in our life, knowing that we can hold nothing back from the fire of love which consumes even those faults which we dearly cherish.

Let us then share these ashes from each other's hands and know that God will surely fulfil the promise of newness within our life.

Philip Freier
Australia

Ash Wednesday Litany

Leader: Trident is the countersign to the cross. It arrogantly threatens to undo the work that the cross has done. By Trident, all things will be destroyed.

Response: **By the cross, all things will be reconciled.**

Leader: The sign of the nuclear age is Trident.

Response: **The sign of Christ is the cross.**

Leader:	In Trident, violence is victorious.
Response:	**In the cross violence is defeated.**
Leader:	In Trident, evil has dominion.
Response:	**In the cross, evil has been overcome.**
Leader:	In Trident, death reigns supreme.
Response:	**In the cross, death has been swallowed up. In this nuclear age, let our sign be the sign of the cross.**

Pax Christi
Britain

A Reflection for Ash Wednesday

Fellow Worker

2 Corinthians 5:20–6:2

Paul calls us co-workers of Jesus Christ. He realizes that we do not always live up to that ideal and he warns that we should not ignore the grace that we have received from God. Yet, he sticks to that description of himself and of the followers of Jesus. We are workers, we are working at something. We can work for money, for pleasure and power, or because we are greedy, selfish or in need.

From a Christian point of view we work to establish God's kingdom on earth.

Action:

Consider all the things you do and don't do in the light of being a co-worker with Jesus Christ. Do you ever make that connection? Are you healing the world by living in it?

(Adapted)

Joseph G. Donders
The Netherlands

Ash Wednesday Liturgy
A Lenten Witness for Peace

Each year an Ash Wednesday Liturgy takes place in London, UK, at Embankment Gardens and The Ministry of Defence, Whitehall, which has as its focus an invitation to repent and resist nuclear weapons. This liturgy is offered in the hope that people in places around the world will use or adapt the liturgy for their own cities and towns, meeting in the places relevant to their own situations. This liturgy makes particular reference to the world situation at March 2003. It is anticipated that people will wish to amend or adapt the wording in those particular places according to the needs of the world in any given year.

Welcome

Leader One:

Grace, mercy and peace to you, my sisters and brothers, from the one true holy God and Jesus Christ our Saviour.

And also with you.

Call to Worship

Leader Two:

This liturgy is dedicated to the inspection of our individual and collective consciences.

Those of us who have put our faith in Jesus, the lamb of God, weep for those who put their faith in nuclear weapons. Theirs is an intolerable idolatry which our action today is intended to remove by whatever means our conscience will allow, in accordance with the Way of Christ, by the power of the Holy Spirit and for the establishment of God's kingdom on earth.

Having made our own act of penitence here we shall go to the Ministry of Defence to call for repentance there, and to mark the place with the Cross of Christ. This will be our gift of hope and holiness for those who have pledged their allegiance to the powers of desolation. To all who walk in darkness and the shadow of death may the power of Christ, crucified and risen, bring light and hope and peace.

Prayer:

Ever-loving living God, you hate nothing you have made and forgive the sins of all who turn to you in penitence and faith. Take from us hearts of stone and give us hearts of flesh, that we may love you with all our soul and our neighbour as our self.
Amen

Song: 'Seek Ye First the Kingdom of God'

Scripture Reading: Matthew 6:1–6, 16–18

A Reflection

Prayer:

O God, you have made us for yourself and against your longing there is no defence. Mark us with your love and release in us a passion for your justice in our disfigured world, that we may turn from our guilt and face you, our heart's desire.
Amen

Blessing of Charcoal and Ash:

Those who have prepared to mark the building come forward with charcoal. The ash and charcoal will be blessed with holy water.

Leader Two:

Dear friends in Christ, let us ask God to bless this charcoal and ash which we will use as a mark of our repentance.

Holy and immortal God you do not desire our death but rather that we should live. Bless this charcoal and ash that it may be for us a sign of repentance and a mark of your salvation through Christ who died for us and rose from the ashes of death to bring us eternal life.

Amen

Act of Penitence

Representatives of groups, e.g. Pax Christi, Christian CND, distribute the ash.

Representative One:

From the dust of the earth we were created.

All: To the dust we shall return.

Representative Two:

Throug' 'r sins we have destroyed and scattered the resourc ᴉf the earth and her children.

May our repentance gather us into a new community, which cherishes the earth and all her people.

Representative Three:

Direct our hearts to better things, O God, heal us from sin and ignorance as we repent and believe the gospel.

People who wish to be marked with the cross should step forward.

Representatives: Repent and believe in the gospel. **Amen**

Chant:] ie, kyrie eleison (Lord, have mercy upon us)

Followed by

Song: 'Spirit of the Living God'

Commissioning

People who have prepared to risk arrest step forward.

Our merciful God gave his son to die for us upon the cross. We who have been marked with the cross send you with God's blessing to be a witness to salvation through Jesus Christ our Lord.

Leader One:

Do not put your trust in princes but trust in God alone.

People who have prepared to risk arrest may leave.

Prayer of Commitment

Leader One:

We pray that our peaceful intentions may be clearly expressed in our worship, in our symbolic acts of witness and in the way that we relate to those we meet this day and throughout Lent – particularly any who may not understand the Christian basis for our action. Let us pray . . .

As members of the body of Christ, we will witness together in various ways at the Ministry of Defence. You are invited to share in the following prayer.

Loving God, inspired by your Holy Spirit, we go to the Ministry of Defence to worship, vigil, fast and pray – and to share in the act of marking the place with ashes and charcoal of repentance.
In undertaking this witness, we commit ourselves to act in a spirit of love and non-violence, in the name of Christ.
Amen

Blessing/Dismissal

Leader Two: Christ be with me.
All: **Christ be within me.**
Leader Two: Christ behind me.
All: **Christ before me.**
Leader Two: Christ beside me.
All: **Christ to win me.**
Leader Two: Christ to comfort and restore me. Christ beneath me.
All: **Christ above me.**
Leader Two: Christ in quiet.
All: **Christ in danger.**
Leader Two: Christ in hearts of all that love me.
All: **Christ in mouth of friend and stranger.**
Leader Two: Let us go in the peace of Christ.
All: **Amen. Thanks be to God.**

Move to Station Two

Song: 'Jubilate, ev'rybody'

Gathering Prayer

Leader Three:

Lord God, we gather like Moses and Miriam and sing with joy, despite the noise of warriors behind us and unknown dangers before us. But your staff leads us on and you feed us with manna from heaven. Give us courage in these forty days of Lent to follow you as the Israelites followed you for forty years through Sinai. May we never fall away from you but live by your commandments, in righteousness and peace all the days of our life.
Amen

Scripture Reading: The Song of Moses, Exodus 15:9–18

11

Reflection

Leader Three:

When Moses and the Israelites had crossed the Red Sea the prophet Miriam took her tambourine and all the women danced as she sang: 'Sing to the Lord, because he has won a glorious victory; God has thrown the horses and their riders into the sea.'

We have heard the song of Moses also, in which the enemy has tried to lay waste the people, taking what they want by the sword. But God's strength is made known in weakness when the defenceless Israelites pass through the sea which swallows up the chariots and weapons of war. So today, we offer praise to God as his people, who refuse the idolatry of nuclear weapons, and renew our covenant with God in whom alone we trust.

All: God forbid that I should boast of anything but the cross of our Lord Jesus Christ, through whom the world is crucified to me. And I to the world.

Scripture Reading: Galatians 6:14

Symbolic Action

The cross is dedicated. People may venerate the cross by coming forward to touch it and then re-mark themselves with the cross on their forehead.

Leader Four: Scripture Reading: 1 Corinthians 1:22–24

All: God forbid that I should boast of anything but the cross of our Lord Jesus Christ through whom the world is crucified to me and I to the world (Galatians 6:14).

Leader Four: Scripture Reading: 1 Corinthians 1:25

Prayer for Peace:

**Lead us from life to death,
From falsehood to truth,
Lead us from despair to hope,
From fear to trust,
Lead us from hate to love,
From war to peace,
Let peace fill our heart,
our world,
our universe.
Amen**

Move to Station Three

(In front of the Ministry of Defence main building)

The cross is held up and people pass under it in silence on the way to the third station.

People who have not yet written a prayer of hope or penitence on paper provided should do so now. It will then be nailed to the cross.

Song: 'Be Still and Know that I Am God'

Gathering Prayer

Leader Five:

Call us, Lord, away from idols, to the true riches of your grace. Keep us true to your commandments that we may learn to love you with all our heart and all our mind and all our strength and our neighbour as ourself.
Amen

Reading: The Covenant is Broken

Leader Six: Scripture Reading: Exodus 32:1–4, 15–21

Reflection

Leader Five:

Moses broke the tablets of stone but the people broke the commandments. 'You shall have no other God but me,' says the Lord. The commandment still holds true – but the idolatry we now face is far more threatening than the idolatries of the past; the golden calf is now made of nuclear and other weapons of mass destruction. To worship it, as nations do, could blow us all to hell.

Yet the people demand that wealth, oil, and the power they attract are set up as gods to be worshipped. Nothing must stand in their way even if nuclear warheads are necessary to defend them. And nuclear weapons themselves are set upon the altar of power, conferring status on Britain, America and other nations, and distorting every agenda in favour of the rich at the expense of the poor. In contrast to this we follow another way. A new covenant has been established and God once more is seen on earth – not in power and glory but in the weakness of an innocent man, nailed to a cross. It is to that cross that we nail our hopes and fears today.

Symbolic Action

Prayers of hope and calls to repentance are nailed to the cross.

Prayer for Peace:

Lead us from life to death . . . *(as p. 13)*

Move to Station Four

(The entrance to the Ministry of Defence Old War Office building)

The cross is carried in procession to the fourth station. People who wish to do so may walk the rest of the way barefoot.

An Appeal for Fasting and Prayer for Peace from Pope John Paul II

Leader Seven:

Dear Brothers and Sisters! For months the international community has been living in great apprehension because of the danger of war that might disturb the whole of the Middle East region and exacerbate the tensions that, unfortunately, are already present at the beginning of the new millennium. It is a duty for believers, regardless of the religion to which they belong, to proclaim that we will never be able to be happy if we are against one another; the future of humanity will never be able to be assured by terrorism and the logic of war.

Leader Eight:

We Christians, in particular, are called to be like guardians of peace in the places where we live and work. We are asked to be alert, so that consciences will not yield to the temptation to egoism, falsehood and violence.

Therefore, I invite you to dedicate with special intensity this Ash Wednesday to prayer and fasting for the cause of peace, especially in the Middle East.

Above all, let us implore God for the conversion of hearts and a generous view in just decisions to resolve with adequate and peaceful means the contests that hamper the pilgrimage of humanity in our time.

This common invocation will be accompanied by fasting as an expression of penance for the hatred and violence that contaminate human relations. Christians share the ancient practice of fasting with many brothers and sisters of other religions, who in this way want to be despoiled of all pride and dispose themselves to receive from God the greatest and most necessary gifts, among which, in particular, is that of peace.

Leader Eight:

From now on, we invoke for this initiative, which is placed at the beginning of Lent, the special assistance of Mary Most Holy, Queen of Peace. Through her intercession, may the evangelical beatitude 'Blessed are the peacemakers, for they shall be called children of God' resonate with a new force in the world and find concrete acceptance.
(Vatican City)

Scripture Readings: Luke 19:41–44; Mark 11:15–17; Mark 13:9–13; Luke 22:19–20

Reflection

Leader Seven:

When Rome was the great superpower of its day, Jesus went up to his capital city – Jerusalem – to lament its compliance with the norms of Roman society, its duplicity and its greed. With him went disciples whom he called out into a renewed covenant with God.

Today in our capital city (London, or name your own capital city or local town), we have re-enacted that calling at a place which symbolizes for us the hypocrisy of those who seek to keep peace, while threatening the world with nuclear war. Now, as an act of covenant, you are invited to kneel at the cross and to pray. You are also welcome to receive wine as a sign of the covenant we share with Christians across the world, who seek peace without threats and believe that God has indeed given us the victory in Jesus Christ our Lord.

A Covenant with Christ

Candles are lit, wine is poured out and distributed and the cross is raised to face the building. Everyone is invited to remove their shoes and kneel in veneration.

Song: 'My Song is Love Unknown' *(kneeling)*

An Acclamation
(standing)

Leader Eight:

Jesus Christ, crucified and risen, assured his disciples that he would be with them to the end of the age.
We are wayfarers, pilgrims following roads to the ends of the earth, on our way to the end of the age.
Behold, I am with you to the end of the age.
We are travellers on the road to freedom – a gracious company with good news for all whom we meet on the way.
Behold, I am with you to the end of the age.
We'll travel lightly and learn as we go. As disciples of Christ, we have no protection though the journey may be hard and long.
Behold, I am with you to the end of the age.
We travel with authority, fearful of none; we are sent to be opponents of evil and heralds of eternal hope.
Behold, I am with you to the end of the age.
We travel with humility as servants of Christ with the cross as our compass to show us the way.
Behold, I am with you to the end of the age.
When the way is uncertain and shadows are sinister – when dangers threaten, we'll not be afraid but take heart because Jesus has said: 'Behold, I am with you to the end of the age.'

A Sharing of Christ's Peace

Leader Eight:

Grace, mercy, righteousness and truth have come from God. Jesus has declared it and the Holy Spirit has made it known. Light shines and the darkness cannot overcome it. The peace of Christ be with you;
and also with you.

Song: 'You Shall Go Out With Joy'

Final Prayer:

Lead us from life to death ... *(as p. 13)*

People may wish to remain for a while in silent prayer.

Liturgy prepared by John Ansell
Pax Christi/Catholic Peace Action/Christian CND
England

Thursday After Ash Wednesday

Human Dignity

Luke 9:22–25

Jesus speaks about the possibility of losing yourself. According to him it is the worst thing that can happen to you. He says that you cannot compensate for that loss even if you gain the whole world.

Some people take those words seriously. There is the person who was making thousands of pounds, maybe even millions, doing work that had no meaning for her. One day it suddenly dawned on her. She changed completely and gave up everything she had to become more fully the person that she is.

The story of St Francis of Assisi is similar. He left his job at his father's shop, gave up all his possessions and set about regaining his real identity. He succeeded and what a joy he has been to the whole world to this day.

There are many others who have redirected their lives in less romantic and dramatic ways. They have changed jobs, altered their personal lives, joined a support group or a self-awareness programme, regaining their dignity and their humanity.

Action:

It is rarely possible to make changes in our lives in the way Francis of Assisi did. It is almost always possible, however, to redirect the work we do, to shift our interests – from those which compromise our dignity and cause us to lose our sense of identity, to those which are more human and more divine.

(Adapted)

Joseph G. Donders
The Netherlands

Friday After Ash Wednesday

Integrity

Isaiah 58:5–8

It is nothing new for those who believe that all people were created by God to be interested in justice. They always have been. It is hardly avoidable. If you believe that all people are created by God out of God's hands, you cannot ignore those who are hungry, naked, abused, or oppressed. Isaiah drew these conclusions from the reading. Writing in the name of God, he says that if we turn away from our brothers and sisters who are in need, we are of no consequence, we lose our integrity. If we do not turn away from them, integrity will go before us; our light will shine like the dawn the world over.

Action:

We are so often caught up in our daily social and work lives that the real depths of ourselves and of others are lost on us. The prophet Isaiah invites us to have a good look at ourselves and others, and to draw conclusions about our lifestyles.

(Adapted)

Joseph G. Donders
The Netherlands

Saturday After Ash Wednesday

Restorer

Isaiah 58:9–12

Again and again we read and hear that the world is falling apart all around us. We might feel like joining in the endlessly repeated refrain: Law and order are falling apart; the good old values are disappearing; our house is ruined; the water has dried up; our strength is dissipated; our old bones are giving way; the shadow hanging over our lives is getting darker and darker.

Awareness of the crisis facing the earth and hunger for change seem to be growing. The prophet speaking in the name of God tells us clearly that we have to take an interest in seeing that justice is done, in providing relief and in honouring God. We have to do this in a new way, a way that is appropriate to our day and age. Then we will be called 'restorers of ruined houses' and 'rebuilders of ancient ruins'.

Action:

It is good to be critical. Considering the situation the world is in, prophets are necessary. Negative criticisms are useless. As Christians we must not be prophets of doom. Are you?

(Adapted)

Joseph G. Donders
The Netherlands

Sackcloth and Ashes

Do you really know what's going on inside me, Lord?
It isn't as straightforward as you'd hope!
I can feel really bad about some of the things going on in my
    head and heart.
Other things, aren't so bad. Sometimes I quite surprise myself.
Some of the surprises are pleasing, some are not.
I guess you're pleased, Lord, sometimes, and often not.

I know Ash Wednesday is the day for repentance, getting
    ready for Lent.
The day of confession.
The day for such a mega-confession that there's nothing left to
    be salvaged.
It is me that's all wrong and it's all of us that are all wrong!

Did Jesus make people feel bad for the sake of it? Was that his
    plan?
Religious professionals did enough of that.
Jesus challenged us to see ourselves and others differently,
more lovingly and less pedantically.
He wanted people on friendly terms with You and
    themselves.
He said to so many, 'So this is who you are, imagine who God
    can see you becoming.'

This Ash Wednesday I'm not just going to make a list of what I,
my community and the world have got wrong.
This Ash Wednesday I'm going to think about just one or two
    situations in
my life, in our world that bother You.
I'm going to imagine how Jesus would talk to me about them,
how he would talk to us about them.
What parables or stories Jesus might tell to help us see things
    from Your holy perspective.
It'll be uncomfortable. I'll have to be honest with him.
I know that there will be confession more profound
than any list I might come up with on my own.
And I know that he will help me move on.
Thanks be to God.

John Ll Humphreys
Wales/Scotland

Part Two

Lent and Passiontide

Into the Wilderness

*'Where can I go from your Spirit? Where can I flee
from your presence? If I go up to the heavens, you are there,
if I make my bed in the depths, you are there.'* (Psalm 139:7–8)

Wilderness

Wilderness is wide.
Bare rocks are there –
No place to hide,
Exposed to all the elements
From every side.

Wilderness holds fear
Of dangers seen, unseen,
From far and near,
Threatening sounds and shadows
Are everywhere.

Wilderness can bloom,
Creative power is there.
Trees and plants find room,
Signs that life will flourish,
Death be overcome.

Wendy Ross-Barker
England

A Wilderness Experience

One aspect of spending time in a wilderness environment is a sensitisation to ecological and evolutionary time. The modern urban lifestyle focuses on the current day and plans a few months ahead. Political and economic leaders are generally geared up to the present and immediate future. However, a wilderness contains rock formations and sands formed over millennia, and creatures which have adapted over many centuries to harsh conditions. A wilderness experience must remind of human reliance on the natural world and provide the time to explore earth's age, beauty and fragility.

If we are truly interested in sustainability we must expand our time frames to consider at least ecological time, if not evolutionary time. It may be that the introduction of a new chemical or technology into the environment can have consequences which are only apparent over decades or centuries. Genetic engineering and nuclear contamination, for example, have the potential to destabilise entire systems and undermine the ability of future generations to meet their needs.

A wilderness experience must engender humility and respect for existing life systems provided by the Creator. A wilderness experience provides silence and the opportunity to hear the spirit of God speak through the natural world.

Ellen Teague
England

A Hymn for Lent

Jesus, who went into the wilderness
To face its dangers and confront its fear,
Hunger and thirst, day's heat and cold of night,
You knew it all – no rest or shelter there.

Jesus, come now into life's wilderness,
Where pain and suffering threaten and dismay,
Walk with your people in life's harshest days,
Give them your courage, take their fear away.

We pray for all who bear the wilderness
Of shattered lives and ruined dreams of peace,
For all who cry for justice to be done,
That your imprisoned ones may know release.

As in the wilderness you made your choice,
Rejecting cunning, rule of force and greed,
Give courage to the powerful and the strong
To dare God's path of love, where you will lead.

Wendy Ross-Barker
England

First Sunday of Lent

Help us, Lord, to face our demons, our powers, as you faced
yours. You were a man of power who could change stones to
bread, conquer kingdoms and fall from the Temple roof
without harm. You spent forty days searching for the way to
use your powers for the coming of the Father's Reign of Peace,
Justice and Holiness. Help us to use our baptismal powers in
the same way. Help us to use our anger at injustice in ways
that will effect change, get things done and give witness in
word and deed to the Reign you so ardently desired. Help us
to use our lust not to abuse or exploit but rather to discover
what are our deeper hungers and thirsts so that from the desert
may bloom justice and peace. Help us to overcome our sloth so
that from indifference we may turn to deep concern for others
who suffer and die because there is no one to turn the stones
of hunger into bread, to build a society founded on justice and
solidarity and to practise true religion which defends the
widow and orphan and gives shelter to the stranger. Amen

Frank Regan
England/Peru

Something for Lent

If you're going to give up something for Lent, what about
    giving up:
Feeling hopeless about the debt of the poorest countries
Tolerating nuclear weapons and arms trading
Wasting water and other resources
Using the car for short journeys

If you're going to do something positive for Lent. Why not:
Befriend asylum seekers and challenge racist remarks
Make a financial commitment to support third world projects
Buy locally produced organic food and fairly traded products
Spend more time with your children

Ellen Teague
England

God of the Unknown

We pray for those who go reluctantly into the unknown –
an elderly woman leaving a life-long home for a flat in
sheltered accommodation,
a man being made redundant from the work that gives
stability and identity –
no choice but to go; into a future unchosen, hope the merest
gleam.

God of the unknown
Walk with them and show them your way.

We pray for those who go with relief into the unknown –
A woman leaving the familiarity of violence and the
struggle to survive,
A refugee escaping torture and prison for an uncertain
existence in a strange land –
Leaving behind the past, for a future hesitantly unfolding
into a new growth.

God of the unknown
Walk with them and show them your way.

We pray for those who go joyfully into the unknown –
a man resuming study, finding new confidence in the
excitement of learning,
a woman taking up a new post, eagerly responding to the
challenge,
stepping forward, into a future bright with possibilities and
the fulfilment of dreams.

God of the unknown
Walk with them and show them your way.

For yours is the past, the present, the future,
and you, mysterious God,
are our familiar companion in the unknown.

Jan Berry
England

Desolation

Faithful and merciful God, we thank you that you are always
there even when we feel that we cannot make contact with you.
We remember with humility how we have been led through
dark patches of our lives when we felt utterly alone and
abandoned. We remember that we expected some dramatic
gesture from you but found you in the stillness. We are sorry
for our lack of faith, for the pride that thinks it all depends on
us. Increase our faith, give us courage to believe even in our
times of doubt, that you are faithful to the Covenant you made
with your people so long ago.

Yorkshire Synod
United Reformed Church

A Prayer of Confession

Forgive us:
    for closing ourselves to the driving of your Holy Spirit;
    for choosing to live in the places of comfort rather than
        being led into the wilderness;
    for letting fear of the person who is different rule our lives
        rather than letting your love for all people fill our hearts;
    for our separation from one another in the Body of Christ;
    for not trusting that you hold the future in your hands.

Elizabeth Welch
England

Desert

Desert
Desert, where there is nothing to hide behind
Desert, with only the sear of extremes.

Sands drift, cover, uncover, recover
All the old order, the palaces of men
Shifting barren landscape with no fixed point
Illusions of shelter.

There was, I know, choice in this
To enter this blinding place with no shelter
But it was not, is not, a choice I welcome.

Oh for the sweet and pleasant martyrdoms
Of giving up chocolate for Lent
Choosing what to deny, with what to mortify the flesh.

But You do not ask us to give, only to choose,
Having chosen . . . Love . . . all else is less
And Love, jealously possesses more, pursues
And desires nothing less.

And I am greedy for the small human pleasures.

Wendy White
England

The Wasteland

Here in the wasteland, where you had not thought to find life,
you will suddenly find the signs of God's renewal, blooming
and flowering and bursting forth from the dry earth with great
energy, God's energy. In the driest month, you will find on the
branches' tips new shoots of life. Under the rock in the desert
will sprout a flower, a delicate bud of the new life.

Jean-Bertrand Aristide
Haiti

Desert Flowers

Even the desert
Will blossom with flowers.
That's what you tell us, Lord.

And in some most desolate
And inhospitable places of this earth
That's how it sometimes is.
In parched, infertile ground
Made thirsty for water
Under an unrelenting sun,
In your season and your time
A great technicolour spectacle of flowers
Bursts forth with unexpected joy,
Surprising the desert landscape
In which it has its roots.

Unlike that multi-coloured carpet
On that hardened sandy floor,
For us, it's maybe different, Lord.
Often your miracles creep up on us quietly
On tiptoe as it were,
Without theatrical drama,
Emerging in your way, your time,
And taking us, quite frankly, by surprise.

Forgive us, Lord
The times we thought you had forgotten us,
The long and barren months of waiting
When we simply failed to see
Beneath the surface of our lives
The quiet, unhurried unfolding
Of your will.

The flowers in the desert, Lord,
Know all your ways.
In your created world it's not unusual

That period of waiting in the dark.
A time when all seems dead,
When absolutely nothing
Gives a hint of what is happening.
But in those parched and barren times,
Seeds are scattered, roots are formed,
The promise of your beauty
Germinating in the dark.

Lord, thank you that you help us
To be patient in the dark,
Thank you that you help us
To wait on You, in trust.

With clarity of hindsight
We now can see that after the desert waiting time
The time of flowering comes.

Lord, germinate the seeds
That you have planted in this church.
Bring forth a great explosion of your joy.
Together help each one of us
To grow as you would wish.

Unfold your great creation
Through your church.

Pat Marsh
England

Meditation and Prayers for Lent

Voice 1: What are you giving up for Lent?
Voice 2: I'm giving up meals out and take-aways, then the
money I save will go towards a holiday abroad, and
I'll get into that dress I bought in the January sales.

Voice 1: All this will be yours if you worship me.
What are you giving up for Lent?

Voice 3: I'm giving up buying magazines, then the time I
would have spent reading them I'll use to decorate
the lounge, and the money I save will go towards
new curtains.

Voice 1: All this will be yours if you worship me.
What are you giving up for Lent?

Voice 4: I'm giving up watching TV and enrolling for a
computer course. That should further my chances
of promotion at work.

Voice 1: All this will be yours if you worship me.

Voice 2: The scripture says, worship the Lord your God, and
serve only him.

Voice 3: Lord God,
Please help us use this time of Lent wisely, as a
period of preparation for Easter, spending more
time reflecting on your word and praying for
spiritual renewal. Instead of 'giving up', may we
'give out' and use our money, time and talents to
serve others, so that your love may shine through
us and be a reflection of you in our lives.

Amen

Voice 4 Saviour Christ,
You never gave up on anybody; you always saw
goodness in people. We remember Mary
Magdalene and Zaccheus, how you reached out to
them and they responded, so that their lives were
turned around.
Thank you for the certainty that you will never give
up on us.

Amen

Voice 2 Holy Spirit,
You led Jesus into the desert and gave him the
power to resist temptation. Be with us and make us

strong when we are tempted to be economical with
the truth, or when we want to put our own interests
first, or when it is easier to stay silent rather than
take the opportunity of speaking about our faith.
Please fill us with your power, so that we are ready
on Easter morning to proclaim the wonder of our
risen Lord.

Amen

Heather Johnston
Scotland

Wait, Wait on Our God

When the land is dry and barren,
Reduced to degraded dust,
Wait for God to restore life,
Bringing growth for our emptiness.

Wait, Wait on Our God,
Keep vigil, keep faith,
for hope comes in the morning.

When the city is derelict,
with boarded-up windows and abandoned cars,
wait for God to restore its vitality,
bringing anger to our numbness.

Wait, Wait on Our God,
Keep vigil, keep faith,
for hope comes in the morning.

When we are numbed with grief,
raw pain breaking the monotony,
wait for God's tender touch
bringing comfort for our healing.

Wait, Wait on Our God,
Keep vigil, keep faith,
for hope comes in the morning.

Jan Berry
England

God of All Humanity

In a world full of fear,
Open our hearts to your love.

Though we walk in desolate valleys.
Open our minds to your hope.

As we seek paths in the darkness,
Open our eyes to your light.

We turn away from hatred,
Towards love.

We turn away from intolerance,
Towards understanding.
As sisters and brothers,
We commit ourselves to compassion.
Together, not alone,
We pray for peace.
Amen

Linda Jones/CAFOD
England

Waiting

I am
waiting:

waiting for God
in the stillness
drawing near to Him
with faith,
sheltering
under the shadow of his wings,
letting Him hold me
very tightly;

content to wait
and pray
and be with God,

content to 'be'
as I wait.

Pat Marsh
England

We Dare to Imagine a World Where . . .

We dare to imagine a world
Where hunger has no chance to show its face
We dare to dream of a world
Where war and terror are afraid to leave their mark
We long to believe in a world
Of hope unchained and lives unfettered
We dare to share in the creation of a world
Where your people break free.

Dare we open our own minds to difference?
Dare we open our own lives to change?

Your kingdom come, O Lord
Your will be done.
Amen

Linda Jones/CAFOD
England

'Man Shall Not Live by Bread Alone'

Turn these stones to bread
what use is that to me?
I need more than bread
to fulfil my ministry.

I need faithful people
to be of use to me
solid as these stones
to fulfil my ministry.

My body is the bread
that you take and consume
My spirit is the stone
rolled from the empty tomb.

Heather Johnston
Scotland

I Believe ... (1)

I believe in the equality of all,
rich and poor.
I believe in liberty.
I believe in humanity, and that through it
we can create unity.
I believe in the love within each of us,
and in the home, happy and healthy.
I believe in the forgiveness of our sins.

I believe that with divine help
we will have the strength to establish
equality in society.
I believe in unity,
the only way to achieve peace, and
I believe that
together we can obtain justice.

Prayer of an Ayacucho Youth group
Peru

I Believe . . . (2)

I believe, Lord, that
everything good in the world
comes from you.
I believe in your great love for all people.
I believe that because you
preached love,
freedom
and justice
you were humiliated
tortured and killed.

I believe that you continue
to suffer in our people
risen in rebellion;
that you are present
In the far off wind
that carries the weeping of the people
the oppressed who seek their imprisoned freedom.

I believe that you
accompany us in waiting for
the dawning of a new day.
I believe that you will give us strength
so that death

does not find us without
having done enough
and that you will rise
in those who have died
seeking a different world.

A Peasant Woman
El Salvador

I Believe ... (3)

I believe that behind the mist the sun waits.
I believe that beyond the dark night
It is raining stars.
I believe in secret volcanoes and the world below.
I believe that this lost ship will reach port.
They will not rob me of hope,
it shall not be broken,
it shall not be broken.
My voice is filled to overflowing
with the desire to sing,
the desire to sing.

I believe in reason and not in force of arms.
I believe that peace will be sown throughout the earth.
I believe in our nobility, created in the image of God,
and with free will reaching for the skies.
They will not rob me of hope,
it shall not be broken,
it shall not be broken.

Source unknown
Chile

Second Sunday of Lent

We stand before you, Father, as a people disfigured by the
sins of injustice committed against the weak and excluded
and against the earth which you have entrusted to us. We long
for a transfiguration which is gift to people fully alive. Open
our ears to the Gospel message of transformation of a society
cleft by divisions of class, race, gender, culture, origin and
religion so that we might live transfigured by a hope that
together we might gradually overcome those divisions. Help
us to reach out to the excluded, the asylum-seeker, the
refugee, the disfigured by social and structural sin so that we
might transfigure their despair and desperation into hope and
peace. Amen

Frank Regan
England/Peru

My Prayer is that I Will Never Become Indifferent

Indifferent to
The wailing of mothers whose babies suck at dry breasts
The whimpers of old people dying of heatstroke with no
    water
The weakness of young people with full-blown AIDS
The screams of children abducted to be child soldiers
The despair of refugees who cannot find a home
The powerlessness of farmers whose fields are full of
    landmines
The smells of open sewers in shanty towns

Indifferent to
The commodification of life through patenting
The alteration of the genetic integrity of plants and animals for
    profit
The destruction of rainforests and unknown species
The pollution of the great oceans

The burden of debt and unequal trade borne by poor
  countries
The threat to the poor of climate change
The legacy of nuclear contamination for future generations

My prayer is that I will never become indifferent.

Ellen Teague
England

Refugees

God, our fellow traveller,
give us courage to leave security behind
that we may take the path of risk
and become your pilgrims.
Give us courage to tread the road of dispossession
that we may reach out to those we meet
and share their load.
And give us grace to listen to those whose voice is lost
that we may hear their cry and shout out for justice.
Amen

Annabel Shilson-Thomas
England

Calling for a Change of Attitude

More than 800 million people still suffer from malnutrition and
it is often difficult to find immediate solutions for improving
these tragic situations. Nevertheless, we must seek them
together so that we will no longer have, side by side, the
starving and the wealthy, the very poor and the very rich, those
who lack the necessary means and others who lavishly waste
them. Such contrasts between poverty and wealth are intolerable for humanity. It is the task of nations, their leaders and
all people of good will to seek every opportunity for a more

equitable sharing of resources, which are not lacking . . . It requires 'firm and persevering determination to commit oneself to the common good' (Sollicitudo Rei Socialis). This spirit calls for a change of attitude and habits with regard to lifestyles and the relationship between resources and goods, as well as an increased awareness of one's neighbour and his legitimate needs.

Pope John Paul II
Vatican City

Money Rules Life

We believe in one God. We should not idolise (make a god of) the market or money. 'At the moment money rules life . . . money comes before Christian values. Through a spirit of co-operation we can make trade work for everyone. The idea must be that my profit is not only my profit, but the fruit of everyone's labours.'

George Anastacio
Mozambique

Conflict

Lord, you chose the way of peace, not war
and urged your disciples to do the same.
Forgive us for the times we have failed to hear your voice
amongst the clamour for power and the rhetoric of war.
In your mercy, look gently on our failure and reassure us of
    your love
as we turn to face our death and prepare for the joy of
    resurrection.
Amen

Annabel Shilson-Thomas
England

Common Welfare

I am an indigenous peasant farmer from the Lenca ethnic group. I mainly grow staple foods and in some seasons, depending on the cycles, I grow potatoes and vegetables to sell both in the local and national markets. I embrace the sustainable agricultural model, under the principle of respect for the environment, culture and life. For us, indigenous people, the land is our mother and we believe it is God's inheritance to all and does not belong to anyone. I believe that we can build a common good together because God has given us things for common welfare to share, such as land, water and wisdom.

Feliciano Martinez
Honduras

Hope and Solidarity

O Lord, giver of light and truth,
deal graciously, we pray, with all who look to you for help.
Uphold us in your love and fill us with your grace
that we may open our eyes and find you in friend and stranger.
In your mercy, join us to one another in solidarity
that together we may become members of the one body
and work in hope towards your kingdom where peace reigns
    with justice.
Amen.

Annabel Shilson-Thomas
England

Don't Call Me a Stranger: The Cry of a Migrant

Don't call me a stranger:
the language I speak sounds different
but the feelings it expresses are the same.

Don't call me a stranger:
I need to communicate,
especially when language is not understood.

Don't call me a stranger:
I need to be together,
especially when loneliness cools my heart.

Don't call me a stranger:
I need to feel at home,
especially when mine is very far away from yours.

Don't call me a stranger:
I need a family because mine I've
left to work for yours.

Don't call me a stranger:
the soil we step on is the same
but mine is not 'the promised land'.

Don't call me a stranger:
the colour of my passport is different
but the colour of our blood is the same.

Don't call me a stranger:
I toil and struggle in your land
and the sweat of our brows is the same.

Don't call me a stranger:
borders, we created them
and the separation that results is the same.

Don't call me a stranger:
I am just your friend
but you do not know yet.

Don't call me a stranger:
we cry for justice and peace in different ways
but our God is the same.

Don't call me a stranger:
Yes! I am a migrant
but our God is the same.

National Council of Churches
India

Prayers of Intercession

Refugees

God, our companion along the road,
Enter with us into the wilderness of uncertainty and the
loneliness of desolation, that through our wanderings and
reflections we too may choose the path of uncertainty and
travel with those who have left behind home and security.

Hear us in your mercy
And strengthen us to do your will.

God, our resistance,
Strengthen our resolve to seek bread which nourishes and
sustains, that through our resistance of instant satisfaction we
may learn to value what we take for granted and seek
solidarity with those who have nothing.

Hear us in your mercy
And strengthen us to do your will.

God, our judge,
Guard us against all arrogance, hypocrisy and self
righteousness, that through choosing the fast that undoes the
fetters of injustice we may share our bread with the hungry
and bring the homeless poor into our house.

Hear us in your mercy
And strengthen us to do your will.

God, our beginning and our end,
Remind us that we are but dust and to dust we shall return,
that through acknowledging our frailty and owning our
mortality we may draw closer to those who live in constant
fear of death.

**Hear us in your mercy
And strengthen us to do your will.**

God, our cross bearer,
Challenge us to take up our cross and to choose the narrow
path, that on our journey we may learn the cost of discipleship
and identify with those who give up home and livelihood for
the sake of principle.

**Hear us in your mercy
And strengthen us to do your will.**

God, our challenger,
Stir up our lives and shatter our complacency, that through
the people we meet and the life stories we share we may be
challenged to change and moved to action.

**Hear us in your mercy,
strengthen us to do your will
And let our lives reflect your purpose.**

Annabel Shilson-Thomas
England

Love Means Deeds

If the hunger of others is not my own,
If the anguish of my neighbours in all its forms
Touches me not,
If the nakedness of my brother or sister
Does not torment me,

46

Then I have no reason to go to church and live.
Life is this: to love one's neighbour as oneself;
This is the commandment of God.
Love means deeds, not good wishes.
For this reason I commit myself to working
For the necessities of my brothers and sisters.

Javier Torres
Nicaragua

The Voice of the Voiceless

O God, may your Church discover and then identify its life
with groups of people who suffer injustice and remain unheard. May your Church be the voice of the voiceless. Let your
Church find them, and struggle with them and so find the way
of your cross and the way to true responsibility.

Emilio Castro
Uruguay

You are the God of the Poor

You are the God of the poor,
the simple and human God,
the God who sweats in the street,
the God with the weather-beaten face.
That's why I talk to you,
in the way that my people talk,
because you are the labourer God,
the worker Christ.

Misa Campesina
Nicaragua

47

Prayers of Intercession

Conflict

For the times we have worshipped power and have succumbed to the temptation of money over justice.

We ask your forgiveness, good Lord.

For the times we have divorced ourselves from the reality of death through believing in 'friendly fire' and 'collateral damage'.

We ask your forgiveness, good Lord.

For the times we have given up something for Lent and remained inert in the face of injustice and war.

We ask your forgiveness, good Lord.

For the times we have pushed ourselves forward at the expense of others and have forgotten your maxim 'the first will be last and the last first'.

We ask your forgiveness, good Lord.

For the times we have been too arrogant to admit to wrongdoing and too proud to seek the path of repentance.

We ask your forgiveness, good Lord.

For the times we have glibly talked about the need for forgiveness and reconciliation without entering into the pain of injustice.

We ask your forgiveness, good Lord.

Annabel Shilson-Thomas
England

Serenade to God

Your balcony beckons
I sing
but my throat
has no note
my guitar has no strings.

Gerald O'Mahony
England

Pray for People

For people in poverty
a state of illiteracy and ignorance.

For people whose labour is less estimated and exploited
because they are unskilled.

For people who have migrated to cities,
other countries and continents
in search of jobs to improve the economic conditions of their
    families
but they are landed in the most strenuous
the dirtiest and lowest paid jobs.

For people who become the victims of well planned tourism
which is a source of joy
and satisfaction for many people.

For people who suffer at the hands of
their in-laws, because of dowry
and other cultural and family traditions.

For people who are suffering in pain and misery
because of illness and malnutrition
due to poverty.

49

For people who are deprived of mutual love
and close bonds of fellowship
because of separation and divorce.

For people who are struggling for dignity
and equality for all people.

For people working in affairs of policy and decision making.

Beulah Shakir
Pakistan

The Temptation to Make Judgements

1 Peter 3:18–22

If we are tempted to make judgements about people living with
HIV/AIDS what does verse 18 say to us?

A Catholic Bishop in Africa came to acknowledge: 'AIDS is a
sickness, not a sin.' Verse 19 points to the promise of resurrection, a theme which runs throughout 1 Peter. That same
promise is there from the start of Lent to its finish on Easter
Day.

Nigel Pounde
Scotland

It is Better . . .

Lord Jesus, it is better to light one candle
than to give up hope
and curse the darkness.
It is better to save one stranger from deportation
and reunite one separated family,
than to say it is not our problem
and we can't do much to help.
It is better to join hands in one work of love
than to sit on our hands and feel powerless.

Lord, help us to love you in the stranger and refugee.
Help us to love ourselves enough to believe
that we can change things for the better.
Help us to love as you have loved us.

Christian Aid

A Litany for Forgiveness

All of us have experienced mental or physical suffering
at the hands of other people.
But each of us has also brought suffering to others.
However, when we are unwilling to forgive,
when we continue to seek revenge,
we deny the essence of God's loving-kindness,
and deprive ourselves of the healing for which our life-force
    longs.

Silence

Forgiveness is a complex process of letting go
which takes time and effort.
It involves letting go of our desire
to suppress our painful memories,
our anger and our shame and being willing
to meet them face to face with love.

Silence

Forgiveness is our most precious gift.
    The most Christ-like blessing we can share.

Forgiveness comes through ceasing to view oneself as an
    unlovable person,
a person whose insecurity leads them to condemn others.

Silence

Forgiveness is our most precious gift.
The most Christ-like blessing we can share.

Forgiveness comes through letting go of the illusion
that we are superior to other people
in our beliefs, attitudes or actions.

Silence

Forgiveness is our most precious gift.
The most Christ-like blessing we can share.

Forgiveness comes through listening
to the story of our oppressors
and experiencing something of their hurt.
Forgiveness grows as we begin to discover something good,
something of God in every human being.
Forgiveness develops as we share our own
vulnerability with them.

Silence

Forgiveness is our most precious gift.
The most Christ-like blessing we can share.

Forgiveness comes through seeing every experience as
an opportunity to learn more about ourselves and
others rather than remain a prisoner of our own history.

Silence

Forgiveness is our most precious gift.
The most Christ-like blessing we can share.

Forgiveness comes through letting go of the idea
that it is solely a matter of feeling sorry for what we have done.
So as well as apologising we seek to change our attitudes
and behaviour, exploring possibilities of righting past wrongs.

Silence

Forgiveness is our most precious gift.
The most Christ-like blessing we can share.

W.L. Wallace
Aotearoa New Zealand

Compassionate God

Open our hearts
That we may feel the breath and play of your Spirit,
Unclench our hands
That we may reach out to one another in openness and
    generosity,
Free our lips
That we may speak for those whose voices are not heard,
Unblock our ears
To hear the cries of the broken-hearted,
And open our eyes
To see Christ in friend and stranger,
That in sharing our love and pain,
Our poverty and prosperity,
We may move towards that peace and justice which comes
    from you
And so be bearers of divine reconciliation.

Annabel Shilson-Thomas
England

We Betray Him by Our Lack of Commitment

Loving God, we continually fail Jesus and his Gospel in so many ways; we betray him by our lack of commitment, by our frightened denials and by our evasion of the responsibilities laid on us.

'God you meet us in our weakness'; strengthen, uphold and correct us when we take the easy way out of the responsibilities laid on us by your son who carried out his responsibilities even to the cross; which proved to be not a defeat but the final triumph over sin and death by his resurrection.
Amen

Yorkshire Synod
United Reformed Church

Words of Forgiveness

Holy God, the rainbow tells of your covenant love for all living creatures, the cross proclaims that love to be without limit. In Christ we are set free from all that binds and burdens us. In his name we are forgiven.
Thanks be to God.
Amen

Elizabeth Welch
England

Pilgrim God

You trod where others dared not tread,
You spoke for those whose voices were not heard
And walked the way of the cross to lay claim to Golgotha.
So lead us through the wilderness of apathy
That our whimpers of despair become cries of protest,
Our faltering footsteps become strides of purpose,

And our blind eyes become visions of hope,
That with the landless of the earth
We may enter Golgotha to songs of resurrection,
Feel its pains turn to birth pangs,
Watch its dry land burst forth and bloom
And hear your pilgrim people rejoice and sing.

Annabel Shilson-Thomas
England

Living Water

John 13:3–15

Water of Cleanliness and Service

When Jesus and his disciples gather for their Passover meal he begins to wash their feet and Peter, as always, makes an impulsive response; first, that he will never let Jesus wash his feet and then that Jesus should wash his hands and head as well.

Afterwards, Jesus gently reminds them all of the need to carry out menial tasks in his service.

Mark 14:22–26

And it is during the Passover supper that Jesus breaks the bread and pours the wine, saying that his body is broken like the bread and his blood poured out like the wine. In this final act Jesus set a pattern which has been at the centre of Christian worship ever since.

Yorkshire Synod
United Reformed Church

Water of joy and water for service are the threads of the above two prayers. We should be always aware of the constant need for clean water in developing countries. Polluted water causes the deaths of many children and adults every day.

Rise Up and Cry Freedom

Holy God,
as you plucked up the people of Israel
and set them down to build and to plan,
so stretch your life-giving hand to the dispossessed,
that with our help they may build and plant,
reap and sow, dance and sing.
Fill them with courage to love,
strength to rebuild and grace to grow,
that once more they may raise up and cry freedom,
may shake off the chains of oppression to wear dignity,
and may leave behind the shackles of despair to embrace hope.

Annabel Shilson-Thomas
England

A Prayer of Dedication

O God, pour out on us the water of life
that we may quench our thirst
and draw our strength from you.
Help us to stand alongside those
who struggle daily for clean water
so that all may be
refreshed and renewed by your love.
Amen.

Christian Aid
England

Every fifteen seconds a child dies from water related diseases.

Water Aid
England

Water Aid helps to provide clean water and sanitation to the world's poorest.

A Sending-Out

God of wonder
Send us out with hearts full of praise
God of wilderness
Send us out with lives full of courage
God of the rainbow covenant
Send us out to live at one with all people
God of the cross and resurrection
Send us out in joyful service.

Elizabeth Welch
England

Vigil Mass for Lent

This Vigil Mass was led by the Bishop of the Clifton Diocese at a CAFOD gathering in 2003, and may be adapted for use at other occasions.

Welcome and Introduction by Bishop or celebrant

Penitential Rite:

Bishop or celebrant:
My sisters and brothers, we are called to be Christ in the world, redeeming it, building up within it the reign of God. Let us pray then in the midst of our Lenten fast, our Lent of repentance and redemption, for our church, and for ourselves who are that church.

We live in a world marked by profound injustice. The vast majority of our sisters and brothers on this earth live in poverty and misery, their human, social and political rights ignored, their dignity daily violated. This is not a consequence of fate or chance, but the result of human behaviour. It is the world we have made.

As church we have often been too afraid, too comfortable, too intimidated, too timid to name the sin of our world. Too often we as church have been part of creating this injustice, either by commission or omission, and this has caused us to fail in our duty to be prophetic. We don't want to be made uncomfortable. We don't want to give up the privileged places we often hold in our world, for we too have sometimes benefited from injustice.

Gathered here, we join together in a prayer of repentance as we ask God's forgiveness so that we may be worthy to bring our gifts to the altar.

Reader: Loving God, when our church, and we who are church, fail to stand with the poor and oppressed peoples who suffer the fruits of injustice – for this we ask your mercy.

Response: **God have mercy on us and on your people.**

Reader: Loving Christ, when our church, and we who are church, allow ourselves to be guided by the criterion of approval or fear of those with power and wealth – for this we ask your mercy.

Response: **God have mercy on us and on your people.**

Reader: Loving God, when our church, and we who are church, fail to address the structures that are at the roots of injustice and violence, when our church, and we who are church, react selfishly to any kind of change – for this we ask your mercy.

Response: **God have mercy on us and on your people.**

Bishop: God of compassion, merciful God, may our prayer of repentance be a point of conversion, turning the hearts of many back to you. This we ask in the name of Jesus our brother and redeemer. Amen.

Opening Prayer:

Father, you have given all peoples one common origin, and your will is to gather them as one family in yourself. Fill the hearts of all with the fire of your love and the desire to ensure justice for all their brothers and sisters. By sharing the good things you give us may we secure justice and equality for every human being, an end to all division, and a human society built on love and peace.

We ask this through our Lord Jesus Christ, your Son, who lives and reigns with you and the Holy Spirit, one God, for ever and ever. **Amen**

First Reading: Genesis 22:1–2, 9–13, 15–18

Responsorial Psalm: Ps 115:10, 15–19; Ps 114:9

Second Reading: Romans 8:31–34

Gospel Acclamation:

From the bright cloud the Father's voice was heard: 'This is my Son, the Beloved. Listen to him.'

Gospel: Mark 9:2–10

Homily

Nicene Creed *or* **Declaration of Faith:**

We believe in God the Father,
who created all the world,
who will unite all things in Christ
and who wants all peoples to live together
as brothers and sisters in one family.

We believe in God the Son,
who became human, died and rose in glory
to reconcile the world to God,
to break down every separating barrier
of race, culture or class,
and to unite all people in one body.
He summons both individual and society,
both the Church and State,
to seek reconciliation and unity between all
and justice and freedom for all.

We believe in God the Holy Spirit,
the pledge of God's coming reign,
who gives the Church power
to proclaim the good news
to all the world,
to love and to serve all people,
to strive for justice and peace,
and to summon all the world to accept God's reign here and
    now.

Amen.

Prayers of Petition:

Bishop or celebrant:	My sisters and brothers, we are called to be a light for our world, a voice that illuminates the darkness of sin and points the way towards overcoming that darkness, the way pointed out to us in this Lenten journey by Jesus of Nazareth. And so we pray with confidence.
Reader:	Loving God, may our church, and we who are church, put ourselves on the side of the poor, on the side of people in need, and strive to give hope to the poor and to defend the cause of the poor.
Response:	**God of our redemption, hear our prayer.**

Reader: Loving God, may we respond to the challenge presented by the poor and oppressed peoples of our world with the speed and boldness adequate to the urgency of our times.

Response: God of our redemption, hear our prayer.

Reader: Loving God, may our church, and we who are church, be faithful to God's covenant of love and offer comfort and support to all who are in need because of illness, poverty and grief.

Response: God of our redemption, hear our prayer.

Reader: Loving God, may our church, and we who are church, overcome the temptation to remain indifferent, and always have the courage to challenge injustice and proclaim the Good News of the Gospel.

Response: God of our redemption, hear our prayer.

Reader: Loving God, may our church, and we who are church, pray in solidarity with our brothers and sisters who live in fear of sickness and death. Through our prayers and actions, may they know the healing comfort of our God.

Response: God of our redemption, hear our prayer.

Reader: Loving God, may our church, and we who are church, work tirelessly for justice and peace. May CAFOD's work, and the work of the whole church, be a visible sign of the glory of God active in the world.

Bishop or celebrant: Loving God, we humbly ask you to receive the prayers of your people. Nourish us with your spirit of hope. Fill our hearts with the zeal to do justice. Help us find that which gives deep meaning for us in the gospel commitment of solidarity with the poor, the work of justice, the witness to truth, to a new creation of abundant life for all your people.

Amen.

Preparation of Gifts:

Bishop or celebrant: Blessed are you, Lord God of all creation. Giver of all that is good. God of peace, God of justice. Through your goodness we have this bread to offer, which earth has given and human hands have made.

Response: **Blessed be God for ever.**

Bishop or celebrant: Blessed are you, Lord God of all creation. Giver of all that is good. God of peace, God of Justice. Through your goodness we have this wine to offer, fruit of the vine and work of human hands. It will become our spiritual drink.

Response: **Blessed be God for ever.**

Bishop or celebrant: Pray my brothers and sisters, that my sacrifice and yours may be acceptable to God, the almighty Father

All: **May the Lord accept the sacrifice at your hands, for the praise and glory of his name, for our good and the good of all his Church.**

Prayer Over the Gifts:

Bishop or celebrant: Lord, hear the prayers of those who call on you and accept the offering of your Church. Fill us with the spirit of the children of God, until all injustice is conquered by love and there is one family, established in your peace. We ask this through Christ, our Lord.

Eucharistic Prayer:

Bishop or celebrant:	The Lord be with you.
All:	**And also with you.**
Bishop or celebrant:	Lift up your hearts.
All:	**We lift them up to the Lord.**
Bishop or celebrant:	Let us give thanks to the Lord.
All:	**It is right to give him thanks and praise.**

Preface:

Jesus, the Compassion of God:

It is truly right to give you thanks,
it is fitting that we offer you praise,
Father of mercy, faithful God.

You sent Jesus Christ, your Son, among us
as redeemer and Lord.
He was moved with Compassion
for the poor and the powerless
for the sick and the sinner;
he made himself neighbour to the oppressed.
By his words and actions
he proclaimed to the world
that you care for us
as a father cares for his children.

And so with all the angels and saints
we sing the joyful song of your praise.

Sanctus

Eucharistic Prayer:

Blessed are you, God of holiness:
you accompany us with love
as we journey through life.
Blessed too is your Son, Jesus Christ,

who is present among us
and whose love gathers us together.
As once he did for his disciples,
Christ now opens the scriptures for us
and breaks the bread:

Great and merciful Father, we ask you:
send down your Holy Spirit
to hallow these gifts of bread and wine.
that they may become for us
the body and blood of our Lord Jesus Christ.

On the eve of his passion and death,
while at the table with those he loved
he took bread and gave you thanks:
he broke the bread,
gave it to his disciples, and said:

Take this all of you and eat it.
This is my body which will be given up for you.

When supper was ended, he took the cup;
again he gave you thanks
and handing the cup to his disciples,
he said:

Take this, all of you, and drink from it.
This is the cup of my blood,
the blood of the new and everlasting covenant
it will be shed for you and for all
so that sins may be forgiven.

Do this in memory of me.

Let us proclaim the mystery of faith.

Acclamation:

And so, Father most holy,
we celebrate the memory of Christ,
your Son,
whom you led through suffering and death on the cross
to the glory of the resurrection
and a place at your right hand.
Until Jesus, our saviour, comes again,
we proclaim the work of your love,
and we offer you the bread of life
and the cup of eternal blessing.

Look with favour on the offering of
your Church in which we show forth
the paschal sacrifice of Christ entrusted to us.
Through the power of your Spirit of love
include us now and forever
among the members of your Son,
whose body and blood we share.

Intercessions:

Lord, perfect your Church
in faith and love,
enliven us with your Spirit
together with
all those your Son has gained for you.

Open our eyes to the needs of all;
inspire us with words and deeds
to comfort those who labour and are burdened;
keep our service of others faithful
to the example and command of Christ.

Let your Church be a living witness
to truth and freedom,
to justice and peace,
that all people may be lifted up
by the hope of a world made new.

Be mindful of our brothers and sisters
who have fallen asleep in the peace
of Christ, and all the dead whose faith
only you can know. Lead them to the fullness
of the resurrection and gladden them with
the light of your face.

When our pilgrimage on earth is complete,
welcome us into your heavenly home
where we shall dwell with you for ever.
There, with Mary, the Virgin Mother of God,
with the apostles, the martyrs,
and all the saints.
we shall praise you and give you glory
through Jesus Christ, your Son.

Through him, with him, in him,
in the unity of the Holy Spirit,
all glory and honour is yours,
Almighty Father.
for ever and ever.

Amen

The Lord's Prayer

Rite of Peace:

Bishop or celebrant:	My sisters and brothers, God has reconciled the world to himself through Jesus his Son and our brother, let us be reconciled one with another.

Let us share Christ's peace and forgiveness and offer each other the sign of peace.

Lamb of God

Communion

Prayer after Communion:

Bishop or celebrant: Lord, you renew us with the one bread that restores the human family to life. By sharing in the sacrament of unity, fill us with a strong and unselfish love that we may work for the progress of all peoples, and lovingly bring your work of justice to perfection. We ask this through Christ our Lord.

Amen

Final blessing:

Bishop or celebrant: Go out and be light. May your word burn like the word of the prophets. May your defence of the poor and suffering, the victims of injustice and oppression, be a transforming power for our world. May your voice, your feet, your hands, become those of Christ, building up the reign of God in our human history. And may God bless us, the Creator, Redeemer, and Breath of our Life.

Amen

Adaptation by Tony Vassallo, CAFOD
England

Mothering Sunday

Now, nobody quite knows.

Is it the parenting or caring?
Is that just by blood parents or adoptive parents?
Should we include foster parents and other carers,
Grandparents and the wider family?
Should we mention other types of families?

Nobody quite knows.

Or should it be the church community?
(We make those promises at baptisms.)
Make sure you include maiden aunts.
Be inclusive.
Teachers and social workers, health care workers,
Sunday school and youth club leaders.
And the uniformed youth organisations?

Nobody quite knows.

And fathers?
Those absent and those present.
(For that matter mothers too.)
Who prays over them? –
Or at least thanks them for their maintenance payments.
Can we thank men for parenting
Without making a joke?

Nobody quite knows.

Or is it what women do?
Should we mention that more women do more work
    for less pay?
Should we mention domestic violence (of both genders)
Or celebrate a woman prime minister, a queen,
Pop stars and actors?

Or should we recognise the many women who work hard
  at work
And in child care and home maintenance?

Nobody quite knows.

And the mother of God?
Not in the Protestant Church.
What about Lydia – the businesswoman
The dealer in purple cloth?
Or Ruth who worked hard in the fields?
Or the other Marys?

Nobody quite knows.

Pat Livingstone
England

My Vicar at Work

It's Mothering Sunday next week.
Is it?
Yes, Easter's early.
How do you know?
My vicar at work,
He told me.

I don't live in the Abbey parish.
Yes you do.
No I don't.
They changed the boundaries.
My vicar at work.
He told me.

Mum, I am getting married.
In church, I hope.
Of course.

You better see our vicar.
First of all I must ask Jim.
My vicar at work.

Change of plan, no church wedding.
Your granny will be upset.
Well we don't go to church.
And I don't know our vicar.
I've talked to Jim.
My vicar at work.

Getting married at Westwick Hall.
A civil ceremony?
Yes, family only, in the morning.
What a disappointment.
Wedding blessing in the afternoon.
Conducted by my vicar from work.

I am not a vicar.
It's in an Anglican colleague's parish.
I am a free church minister.
A chaplain visiting the work place.
For many I am the church.
Their vicar at work.

Y. Mochyn Daear
England

Passiontide
Dying We Live

'Out of the depths I cry to you, O Lord.' (Psalm 130:1)

Passiontide

Take your place, child,
Take your full place in the world.
You deserve to be here
There's no more to fear.
Take your place, child, show your face.

Show your face, child,
Show your full face to the world.
You deserve to be seen,
No more reason to hide.
Show your face, child, there's no disgrace.

No disgrace, child,
No more disgrace in the world.
You deserve to stand tall
Speak your truth out for all,
There's no disgrace, child, speak your truth.

Speak your truth, child,
Speak the whole truth to the world.
I was held down and raped,
Hand clamped hard on my face.
Speak your truth, child, breathe your breath.

Breathe your breath, child,
Breathe your full, deep breaths in the world.
You can open your mouth,
You are free to shout out.
Breathe your breath, child, speak your heart.

Speak your heart, child,
Speak your full heart to the world.
You are free to love true,
No more shackles for you.
Speak your heart, child, love your world.

Sarah Ingle
England

Reflection on the Scales of Justice

Amos 8:4–7

Our choice could
tip the balance
in favour of the poor
and lighten the load
of those weighed down

We could level inequality
and distribute warehouse mountains
Share out the wealth
that was never ours to hoard
Turn the tables
on those who play
the markets
We could stockpile generosity
and speculate in hope
Sell up our shares in selfishness
and settle for the dividends
of solidarity

For added value
build portfolios of justice
or an ISA in the growth
of the kingdom of God
Buy shares in trust and act in faith
Risk our securities to find a richer life

May the percentage of our interest
In people rise
and may we be the prophets
of hope

Sophie Stanes/CAFOD
England

Refugee

Based on a true story from Uganda

How can I tell you my name?
I who have seen
my fellow man in his deepest shame.
I who can tell you of his obscenities.
For I have seen him in the night
come to murder and destroy
all that was precious in my sight,
all that gave my family joy.
And why? What did we do?
We did not rise up against their rule;
we only spoke of what was true
and would not countenance the cruel.
But when corruption wears the crown
then those who dare to say 'This is not right'
become a danger to be put down

So Christians vanish in the night,
for evil cannot face the day,
nor wickedness be seen for what it does.
We all lived in fear and some chose to obey
the orders that deprave the soul.
We cried for justice, but their violation
of our lives is unseen by the law,
for it must serve the rulers of the nation
and all that we have seen it never saw.
No one from my old school now lives at home

and only ten from eighty-two survive
as rootless, nationless we roam,
thankful to God that we were kept alive.
Yet guilty too, and sleepless still
for our eyes always scour the night
because we are the witnesses they failed to kill,
our tongues can speak, our eyes have sight.
So I live here, a refugee,
not from a famine, war nor flood,
But for my faith, my Christianity,
for doing what I knew was good.
Even so I fight my human nature,
holding to grace and life as it should be,
and stifling the angry vengeful creature
that roars within the very heart of me.

Only by the power of faith in a crucified and tortured
    Lord
can I share in the love that conquers death
and understand how hope springs from his blood.
Such is the gift of love
That presidents must tremble, evil be confused
for life does rise and rise again to prove
that truth and hope survive however badly used.

And I forgive,
my brothers did not know
except that they too wanted to survive
and chose that way to follow.
And I forgive,
or else I shall be murdered by their shame.
The memory of their deeds will live.
I do not need to speak my name.

Colin Ferguson
England

Torn Shirt

Torn shirt, no shoes,
My brother.
Hungry, he touches my heart
and I ache to understand, to see,
to feel, to reach,
to share his life,
his laugh, his dance.
I even drink the coffee that he grows,
And smell the flowers he picks,
My brother,
Lord,
May his hunger change my heart.

God of compassion,
I see him now,
Torn shirt, no shoes,
My brother.

Our lives meet in the global market,
Woven together in the web of trade.

But he's hungry,
He touches my heart
And I ache to understand,
To share his life,
his laugh, his dance.

God of compassion and justice,
May such hunger change my heart.

Linda Jones/CAFOD
England

Tiny Coffins

Tiny coffins affect priests at funerals of South African AIDS victims.

Oblate Father Frans Samyn spends most of his Saturdays officiating at three or four funerals.

'The most I did one Saturday was six,' he says. Overwhelmingly, the services are for those who succumb to HIV/AIDS. 'But they don't call it (AIDS) here among themselves,' says the 73-year-old Belgian cleric who came to South Africa in 1957. 'They call it double pneumonia or TB (tuberculosis).' Father Samyn's ministry in Orkney, a mining town in central South Africa, includes serving as pastor of four big congregations and eleven smaller ones. The South African government estimates 1,700 people are infected daily with HIV, the virus that causes AIDS. 'That's 50,000 new cases a month,' Father Samyn says, 'and those are the official statistics.' Many believe the real, unofficial count is much higher.

The tiny coffins that contain the bodies of children are especially sad for Father Samyn. Many of the children come from a child-care centre, funded by money from Belgium and the USA. The centre is the only building in the area with landscaping and a painted exterior. Inside, colourful plastic chairs dot the living room. The 260 children range from toddlers to 18 year olds and most are orphans whose parents have already died of AIDS. All of them have the HIV virus. Father Samyn oversees the project. The annual budget of $12,400 covers food, burial costs, and sewing and woodworking machines for the older children, who learn crafts to support themselves. 'I pray every day for healing for them,' he says.

Source unknown
South Africa

Share in the Suffering of Christ

Hebrews 5:5–10

Our example is Jesus, who in his earthly life identified in total solidarity with the life and suffering of people wherever they were. In today's terms, Jesus is there at truck stops on the trunk roads of India where drivers eye up the local women; Jesus is there sharing a drink and a laugh in his local gay bar in Scotland; Jesus is there in the poverty and violence of shattered African communities. Wherever the HIV virus can spread Jesus is there, reverently submitting, so that his prayers are heard. If there is to be a 'new' High Priest, he has to be one who comes out of the Holy of Holies, out of the Temple precinct even, to touch all of humanity. That is the Church's way to renewal too.

Nigel Pounde
Scotland

The Hand

Inspired by a newspaper photograph of a massacre in Rwanda

Pointing from the rubble and the bones
that once was family and home,
she makes her judgement on a world
full of intention and strong words
at what to sense was senselessness,
to logic a wilderness.

Once she fed her children, rocked a cot,
held and hugged the hurt,
taught the questioning child,
stopped them when they got too wild,
nursed them when they were ill
and would have done so still.

Now she reaches to the mother in us all,
and from her silence powerfully she calls,
my children's future is with you
and all depends on what you do
to take the poison from the feast
and find our children in the beast.

She points from grave into tomorrow,
points to life from death's dark sorrow,
to when the killings have to cease
and children have to make the peace,
fed by faith in which she died
that life shall win and death shall be defied.

Colin Ferguson
England

Sharing Suffering and Compassion

An extract from Sacred Energy – Mass of the Universe

Now we imagine what it is like to be a marginalised
or repressed human being
  what it is like to be stereotyped and judged by society
    in a way that does violence to oneself as a human being
        a gay man or lesbian woman,
        a political activist,
        an avant-garde artist,
        a convicted criminal.

Silence

What it is like to be caught in the poverty trap
with apparently no way out
Except resorting to violence or illegal activity.

Silence

What it is like to have one's culture destroyed
and not to know who one really is.

Silence

What it is like to be maimed in body or mind –
to have lost a part of oneself.

Silence

What it is like to be in a spiritual wilderness
where old beliefs have died and there are as yet no
   replacements,
no resurrection from the tomb.

Silence

May the nurturing fire of compassion
melt the ice of our hearts
the ice of indifference
the ice of imagined superiority
the ice of cynicism and despair.

Let us walk gently with our pain
walk gently with the pain of the world
and join the dance of transforming love
the dance of the wide-eyed pilgrim –
the justice and peace pioneer.
Amen

W. L. Wallace
Aotearoa New Zealand

May Your Kingdom Come

A prayer for refugees

May fear strike no longer,
Let pain fade away,
May earthly power be challenged,
When it plunders the poor,
And tramples on hope.

God of peace, may your kingdom come.

Help us to put away the weapons of war.
Help us to destroy the tools of destruction,
Let earthly power be challenged,
When it plunders the poor,
And tramples on hope.

God of peace, may your kingdom come.

Teach us to follow the ways of justice,
Teach us to walk the paths of truth,
Let integrity challenge the power that plunders,
When it tramples the poor
And pours scorn on our hope.

God of peace may your kingdom come.

Bring peace sweet as honey,
Bring peace like a shield,
And may we be the challenge
To earthly power that plunders
And tramples on hope.

God of peace, may your kingdom come.

Linda Jones/CAFOD
England

Hope, Thanks and Solidarity

Thank you, God, because you have given us everything we have. We have nothing except what you have given us. We worship you with our mouths. We worship you with our bodies. We worship you with everything we have because only you have given us everything. We say thank you today and tomorrow and all days. We do not tire in giving thanks to you.
Amen

A Masai Prayer

Passion for Justice

Give us the confidence to challenge injustice
And to nurture the flame of justice until it burns brightly.

And may the Spirit of Justice and community
Accompany you and light your way.

May this Spirit move you, heal you,
Guide you and challenge you
Call you to action and to prayer.

May this passion for justice burn through you and in you
And may it warm the hearts of those around you
Encouraging hope and overcoming fear.
Amen

CAFOD
England

Fill Me with Compassion

Lord God, help me to love you with my whole heart and my neighbour for your sake. When I see in other people the needs of poverty, loneliness, depression, may I see also your presence in them. Let the fragrance of your perfect love purify me and fill me with compassion.

Raymond Chapman
England

Interview with a Refugee Woman

Milka Lounic is from Drnis in Dalmatia. She tells her story as she weaves a cushion cover featuring St Paraskeva to be used in the refugee centre.

'I left Croatia during Operation Storm. Most of us left – the ones who were left behind were killed. We came here in a convoy in 1995 with my four sons. We brought nothing with us – only our clothes. Some people left without their shoes. We left quickly because of the danger – we just wanted to survive.

I said goodbye to my brothers in front of my house and left for Banja Luka in Bosnia – we had not time to pick up anything. My brothers stayed behind – to this day I don't know what happened to them. Some people know but they will not admit that they have been killed. There are lots of unmarked graves.

I now live with my cousins in Belgrade and my sons come to visit me. They can't help me financially but the greatest gift to me is that they are alive.

The centre provides comfort, chat, a social life. I have fun here. We share the same destiny. Mostly I come on Saturdays but it depends on what the jobs are. I knit sweaters and other clothes for the family. We get wool to make things for ourselves and for the centre to sell.'

Milka Lounic has faith. 'I go to church occasionally. It gives me strength. I was brought up with God. My saint is St Paraskeva (St Friday), a female saint. She's a protector for me

82

and my family and I feel I owe her because when my son had an accident it was just before her saint's day and I think she saved his life.

I have a book about her with special prayers in it. The prayer I learned as a child was:

Holy St Petka
Pray to God in our name
He who is dedicated to you
You will never leave alone.'

Irena Dzajkovska and Ana Simic, co-ordinators of the refugee centre, are pleased to have this story published.

CAFOD
England

Jerusalem Triptych

A Reflective Meditation for Passiontide

Peter

It's hot. It's dusty. I'm thirsty but still we walk. We've been walking for three years now. And I still don't know this man I follow.

We're approaching Jerusalem. The closer we get, the gloomier he gets. It worries me. He keeps muttering about death and when he's gone.

If it were anyone else I'd say they were just being melodramatic. This is different. He's the Rabbi, the Master. What would we do without him?

The others might fall apart if trouble comes, but I'd stick by him. I would never walk away from him!

'Peter', he says and smiles, 'Come on. I'll wash your tired feet when we get there.'

As if! I laugh at his little joke and keep walking.

Judas

It's hot. It is dusty. I am uncertain but still we walk. We have been walking for three years now. Who is this man I follow?

We are approaching Jerusalem. We have travelled together and I have seen miracles. People love him. Hope and expectation shines in their eyes as they gather and talk of him. Crowds follow – they are desperate for him to perform. This is becoming a circus, a freak show. I am uncomfortable and claustrophobic under the weight of all their neediness.

Everything seems upside-down. Just when I think he'll follow some kind of sensible path, he does the opposite. Daily, definitions are turned on their heads.

He has made enemies. He is upsetting the wealthy, the powerful – the very ones he should be courting as allies. Idiot!

This journey to Jerusalem is a death march. I love him. I hate him. He drives me mad. He is mad! This must end.

I make my plans, laugh at some joke, and keep walking.

Jesus

It's hot. It's dusty. I've been walking all my life! And now, near the end-point of this journey, there are so many questions.

We are approaching Jerusalem. There I will ride into the city on the donkey that awaits me. The crowds will cheer in hopeful expectation of . . . what? An uprising? Upheaval? A restoration to former glory days? The crowds will cheer and completely miss the point of my mission and message.

Even now, I have the power to choose. We could disband. I could go back home and be a carpenter once more. There in the bitterness of broken dreams and shattered expectations, I'd spend the rest of my days gnawed at by failure and regret. Foxes have holes and birds have nests, but I no longer have claim on a place to rest. I can't go back, only onward.

Judas doubts and is uncertain. I see him watching me, hoping that I'll fuel his ambition. I am the kiss of death to his dreams. He will betray me.

Peter blusters and is too certain. When the cheers turn to jeers, he'll fall from that pedestal of certainty. He will deny me.

Betrayal, denial, death await. Father, this is a hard road to travel!

Steady, steady. We're nearly there now. They've gone to fetch the donkey that will lead me to my doom. I shrug off the darkness, laugh, and keep walking.

Questions for guided meditation on the above passages

1 You are hot, dusty and thirsty. You are walking the road with Jesus. What does it feel like to be walking with this group?
2 As you walk, where are you – in the middle of the group, at the back, on the edge, or walking near Jesus up at the front?
3 Wherever you are in the group, now move closer to Jesus – he is beckoning to you. What is he saying to you?
4 What would you like to say to him?

If you wish, you may like to finish with the Bible passage – Mark 11:1–11: The Triumphal Entry into Jerusalem.

Suggestions for facilitating meditation – leave a small space between each reflection.

Reflection questions – the questions are provided for people who may be new to silent contemplation, and help to act as a focus. Leave several minutes between the questions.

Nikki Macdonald
Scotland

At the Foot of the Cross

*This order of service was designed for use in Passion Week
at the Ecumenical Centre, Geneva, Switzerland*

Invocation

Leader:

Golgotha is not only a place and an occasion in history but it is a spiritual reality in all times and all places. The cross is not only an instrument of death, but also the key to the mystery of life.

Here, at the foot of the cross, we come face to face with love, and each can learn to make answer to that love.

It is a meeting place; an event that calls for response.

Song

Silence

Bible Reading: Luke 23, 27:32–49

Meditation

Litany

Leader: Let us join in a litany at the foot of the cross.

Merciful God,
We meet each other today, at the foot of the cross,
as inhabitants of one world.
We wait with each other as those who inflict wounds
on one another:
All: **be merciful to us.**
Leader: As those who deny justice to others:
All: **be merciful to us.**

Leader:	As those who put our trust in power:
All:	**be merciful to us.**
Leader:	As those who are greedy:
All:	**be merciful to us.**
Leader:	As those who put others on trial:
All:	**be merciful to us.**
Leader:	As those who refuse to receive:
All:	**be merciful to us.**
Leader:	As those who are afraid of the world's torment:
All:	**be merciful to us.**

Silence

Leader:	Bearer of all pain, we come to share with you the burden of all this world's suffering. We stand by you In the refugee camp:
All:	**we wait and weep.**
Leader:	At the door of the torture chamber:
All:	**we wait and weep.**
Leader:	In the shanty town:
All:	**we wait and weep.**
Leader:	Among the broken street children:
All:	**we wait and weep.**
Leader:	In the oppressor's court:
All:	**we wait and weep.**
Leader:	In the devastated city:
All:	**we wait and weep.**
Leader:	On earth soaked with blood:
All:	**we wait and weep.**

Silence

Leader:	Giver of life, we wait with you to offer the hope that comes from the cross to earth's darkest places. Where pain is deep and affection is denied:
All:	**let love break through.**

Leader:	Where justice is destroyed:
All:	**let sensitivity to right spring up.**
Leader:	Where hope is crucified:
All:	**let faith persist.**
Leader:	Where peace has no chance:
All:	**let passion live on.**
Leader:	Where truth is trampled underfoot:
All:	**let the struggle continue.**
Leader:	Where fear paralyzes:
All:	**let forgiveness break through.**
Leader:	Eternal God, reach into the silent darkness of our souls with the radiance of the cross. O you who are the bearer of all pain:
All:	**have mercy on us.**
Leader:	Giver of life:
All:	**have mercy on us.**
Leader:	Merciful God:
All:	**have mercy on us.**

Song

Benediction

Leader:	May God, who gives us a new vision of life through the Cross, enlighten our understanding, inflame our affections and enable us to walk the way of the cross. And may the love of God, the Father, Son and the Holy Spirit surround us as we seek to discern that love.
All:	**Amen**

World Council of Churches

88

Were You There When They Crucified My Lord?

Jesus is condemned to death

That Friday, the people of Jerusalem faltered, taken unawares,
urged on by spin doctoring, they rallied one cry – 'crucify him'.
That Friday is contemporary, all too frequently repeated.
For the miscarriages of justice that condemn all asylum
seekers as 'bogus'.
Lord have mercy.

Jesus carries His Cross

The cross has no handle or convenient carrier wheels, it had to
be hoisted, pulled and dragged by a staggering man.
Displaced, evicted people know the weight of wood and the
condemnation of indiscriminate bombardment.
Lord have mercy.

Jesus falls

The shadow of the Cross drags heavily against the status quo.
How vulnerable, exposed and helpless people are when lying
under the weight of forced migration and rejection.
Lord have mercy.

Jesus meets His mother

She suffers Your suffering without cradling You; she is
co-redeeming without averting her gaze from pain and
humiliation.
May we, with Mary, never avert our eyes from the stranger
we meet upon the way.
Be our inspiration.

Simon helps Jesus carry His Cross

Man of Africa, your continent once provided a haven for
Jesus' family and now you are called to share His burden.

Inspire us to accompany refugees, many of whom carry the burden of happening to be in the wrong place at the wrong time.
Be our inspiration.

Veronica wipes the face of Jesus

On the blank cloth of yesterday's hopes, that was woven out of dreams and anticipation, is the indelible face 'of the one we seek'.
May we seek Your face in the exile, among the exploited and the scarred, reweave a cloth of hope, fresh for Your imprint.
Be our inspiration.

Jesus falls again

Jesus is the man for all seasons; he stumbled, fumbled and constantly picked himself up along the way.
Dispossessed, forced on a journey without definite destination, the involuntary pilgrim stumbles, fumbles and needs someone to pick them up.
May we be there.

Jesus speaks to the women

Grief without feeling, weeping women, paid mourners, offer little consolation. Jesus bids them mourn not from custom but for the pain on the pavement to Calvary, where lonely women, the majority of the world's refugees mourn their losses.
May we be there.

Jesus falls yet again

In the blood drops, dripping along the way
Jesus rewrites the story of human regeneration.
In the blood-stained patterns of former footprints may all uprooted people be rerouted.
May we be there.

Jesus is stripped

Our fleeced Lamb marked for slaughter and bearing our
blankets of pain,
swaddles us in a blanket of care.
We remember refugees rendered homeless and without:
dependent upon recycled and discarded clothing
to soften bruised bodies and spirits.
Were you there when they crucified my Lord?

Jesus is crucified

They pinned open hands that were always open, healing,
comforting and bringing life.
They stayed two pilgrim feet, which 'went about doing good',
imprints that seal your-love-that-seals.
Were you there when they crucified my Lord?

Jesus dies

What cradle song is sung to awaken Him from the night of the
tomb?
Croon not for me but for Rwandan, Kosovar, East Timorese
and Kurd whose death-pain of abandonment stems from
ethnic cleansing.
Were you there when they crucified my Lord?

Jesus is taken down from the Cross

The place of weakness is also the place of our rising.
Wood is enduring whether plank of shelter or deep sunk
roots.
The tomb and the womb share deep secrets of life-loving
potential.
May hidden, forgotten migrants meet people-of-rising.
On you rests our hope.

Jesus is buried

Falling and failing hearts
are human pain.
Staying on the ground
Is folly for believers.
On you rests our hope.

Jesus rises

Jesus resists containment;
the stones of detention are rolled back,
the border stones peal away
and cleft contained doves sing:
glory to God in the highest and peace to all.
Amen

Mairead Butterly
England

Stations of the Cross
Debt and Jubilee

Welcome and Introduction

Leader:

'Whatever the detailed history of today's debt-ridden countries
. . . those who could be blamed least, the poorest people in the
poorest countries have suffered most.' These words of Cardinal
Hume, together with Pope John Paul II's call to all Christians to
raise their voices on behalf of the poor, are a profound challenge
to us all.

As we meditate on Christ's suffering and death we remember
too those who are suffering and dying today. As we remember
Christ's Resurrection we look for signs of hope and new life in
a changed world.

Mulima Kufekisa from Zambia speaks out, 'What sort of economic justice is it, where those who can afford the least are expected to give to those who already have the most? Enough is enough. It's time for justice.'

Today we ask for the strength, determination and courage to continue to pray and work for justice for all God's people.

All:

Jesus, our friend and our brother, through your life and your journey to the Cross, your death and Resurrection, you have shown us how to live in love. May we always follow your example, living a life of compassion, in the search for peace through justice for all your people.

1 Jesus is Condemned to Death

Reading: Matthew 27:22–26

Pilate said to them, 'What am I to do with Jesus who is called Christ?' They all said, 'Let him be crucified!' 'Why?' he asked, 'What harm has he done?' But they shouted all the louder, 'Let him be crucified!' Then Pilate saw that he was making no impression, that in fact a riot was imminent. So he took some water and washed his hands in front of the crowd. He ordered Jesus to be first scourged and then handed over to be crucified.

Silence

Reading: Today Jesus is Condemned to Death

David Hamalambo is seven years old. He is dying of malaria. It's a treatable disease, but his parents Joni and Rosemary are farmers in rural Zambia, who can't afford medicines or the fee at the clinic.

Silence

Reading

In Zambia, one in five children dies before its fifth birthday. Zambia spends three times as much on debt interest as on health care.

Prayer

All:

Jesus, our friend and our brother, through your life and your journey to the Cross, your death and Resurrection, you have shown us how to live in love. May we always follow your example, living a life of compassion, in the search for peace through justice for all your people.

2 Jesus Carries His Cross

Reading

They stripped Jesus and made him wear a scarlet cloak, and having twisted some thorns into a crown they put this on his head and placed a reed in his right hand. To make fun of him they knelt to him saying, 'Hail, King of the Jews!' ... And when they had finished making fun of him, they took off the cloak and dressed him in his own clothes and led him away to crucify him.
(Matthew 27:28–31)

Silence

Reading: Today Jesus Carries His Cross

Fatoma has no donkey to help her with her load. In a truly impressive display of strength and flexibility she bends to make a flat back parallel to the ground, hoists the heavy 20-litre jerry can into place and then flips a shawl up behind her over the can, tying it in place around her middle. When the jerry can is secure, she stands up, bowed by the weight. She is also carrying her baby, Abdi. She explains that she walks back to her village, Kcheba, which is quite close by. There she leaves the water and, still carrying the baby, comes back for her cow which is drinking at the cattle trough.

Silence

Reading

In Ethiopia a majority of rural women and children spend three to four hours per day collecting unsafe water from open pools and rivers. Many become ill, but Ethiopia only spends just over two per cent of its income on health care. Ethiopia's debt is £3 billion.

Prayer

All:

Jesus, our friend and our brother, through your life and your journey to the Cross, your death and Resurrection, you have shown us how to live in love. May we always follow your example, living a life of compassion, in the search for peace through justice for all your people.

3 Jesus Falls the First Time

Reading

Here is my servant whom I uphold,
my chosen one in whom my soul delights.
I have endowed him with my spirit
That he may bring true justice to the nations.

He does not cry out or shout aloud,
Or make his voice heard in the streets,
He does not break the crushed reed,
Nor quench the wavering flame.
(Isaiah 42:1–3)

Silence

Reading: Today Jesus Falls the First Time

Choma is twelve. His father has just lost his job as a bus driver. Now Choma's family cannot afford to send him to school. The fees are too expensive. Choma lives on the streets, begging, running errands and tending cars. Without education his future is uncertain.

Silence

Reading

Zambia spends five times as much on debt interest as education. Fewer then half of Zambian children go to school, because their parents can't afford the fees.

Prayer

All:

Jesus, our friend and our brother, through your life and your journey to the Cross, your death and Resurrection, you have shown us how to live in love. May we always follow your example, living a life of compassion, in the search for peace through justice for all your people.

4 Jesus Meets His Mother Mary

Reading:

As the child's father and mother stood there wondering at the things that were being said about him, Simeon blessed them and said to Mary his mother, 'You see this child; he is destined for the fall and rising of many in Israel, destined to be a sign that is rejected – and a sword will pierce your own soul too – so that the secret thoughts of many may be laid bare.'
(Luke 2:33–35)

Near the cross of Jesus stood his mother and his mother's sister, Mary the wife of Clopas, and Mary of Magdala. Seeing his mother and the disciple he loved standing near her, Jesus said to his mother, 'Woman, this is your son.' Then to the disciple he said, 'This is your mother.'
(John 19:25–26)

Silence

Reading: Today Jesus Meets His Mother Mary

Aysha, who is around 45–50, has eight children, six girls and two boys. She has given birth to three sets of twins. But when I asked her if she had had any other children who had died, the answer was eight. They mostly died before making it to their second birthday.

Silence

Reading

Nearly half of all children under five in Ethiopia are underweight. One in five Ethiopian children dies before their fifth birthday.

Prayer

All:

Jesus, our friend and our brother, through your life and your journey to the Cross, your death and Resurrection, you have shown us how to live in love. May we always follow your example, living a life of compassion, in the search for peace through justice for all your people.

5 Simon of Cyrene Helps Jesus Carry His Cross

Reading

They led Jesus out to crucify him. They enlisted a passer-by, Simon of Cyrene, father of Alexander and Rufus, who was coming in from the country, to carry his cross.
(Mark 15:21)

Silence

Reading: Today Simon Helps Jesus Carry His Cross

Porfirio Triminio always loved to draw, but he never dreamt he would be able to study art, let alone teach it. Like all his friends, Porfirio thought he would leave school early to support his family, by shining shoes or selling gum on the streets of Esteli in northern Nicaragua.

'Once out of the school system they never go back,' says Daniel Hopewell, who runs mural workshops for children in Esteli. 'They start working and that's it.'

Some murals display a mature grasp of Nicaragua's economic problems. One painting of a health centre depicts a nurse telling children, 'I'm sorry, there are no medicines'. And children protesting, 'We have the right to health.'

Porfirio is now a teacher at the mural workshops. He says they were a wonderful opportunity for him: 'They helped me get to know people and gave me a way into society. Now I want to pass on the talents and confidence I've learnt to other children.'

Silence

Reading

Nicaragua's debt is £5.5 billion, that is £1,334 per person. On average Nicaraguans earn £250 a year.

Prayer

All:

Jesus, our friend and our brother, through your life and your journey to the Cross, your death and Resurrection, you have shown us how to live in love. May we always follow your example, living a life of compassion, in the search for peace through justice for all your people.

6 Veronica Wipes the Face of Jesus

Reading

As the crowds were appalled on seeing him – so disfigured did he look that he seemed no longer human – so will the crowds be astonished at him, and kings stand speechless before him . . .
(Isaiah 52:14–15)

Then from behind him came a woman, who had suffered from a haemorrhage for twelve years, and she touched the fringe of his cloak, for she said to herself, 'If only I can touch his cloak I shall be well again.' Jesus turned round and saw her; and he said to her, 'Courage, my daughter, your faith has restored you to health.'
(Matthew 9:20–22)

Silence

Reading: Today Veronica Wipes the Face of Jesus

Mulima Kufekisa is 28. She runs an organisation that monitors the effects of debt on people in Zambia. She says, 'I believe in working to change unfair situations. Unnecessary suffering saddens me. My dream for the next millennium is debt cancellation so that poor people's lives can be improved.'

Silence

Reading

Out of every £10 Zambia receives in aid, £7 is used to pay interest on debts to rich countries.

Prayer

All:

Jesus, our friend and our brother, through your life and your journey to the Cross, your death and Resurrection, you have shown us how to live in love. May we always follow your example, living a life of compassion, in the search for peace through justice for all your people.

7 Jesus Falls the Second Time

Reading

Without beauty, without majesty we saw him
no looks to attract our eyes;
a thing despised and rejected,
a man of sorrows and familiar with suffering,
a man to make people screen their faces;
he was despised and we took no account of him . . .
By force and by law he was taken; would anyone plead his
    cause?
(Isaiah 53:2–3, 7)

Silence

Reading: Today Jesus Falls the Second Time

Azon is a garment worker in the Philippines, earning £3.60 a day. She had managed to save some money, thinking that she would start her own business if the factory closed down. But she became ill and had to spend all her savings to pay for an operation.

Marilou works at the Golden Thimble factory in Manila, making garments for export. At 32, her working life in the garment industry is almost over. She is on a five-month contract. She says: 'I've worked in the garment industry since I left school at 18. At first I was a regular in the Glorious Sun factory. It's better to be a regular, to have the benefits, the job security.

The five-month limit is awful; you're always worrying about the next job. I'm 32 now, and once I'm 35, I'll be over the age limit.'

Silence

Reading

Countries in debt have to attract foreign investment so that they can earn money to pay the interest. Working conditions often get worse as poor countries compete against each other.

Prayer

All:

Jesus, our friend and our brother, through your life and your journey to the Cross, your death and Resurrection, you have shown us how to live in love. May we always follow your example, living a life of compassion, in the search for peace through justice for all your people.

8 Jesus Speaks to the Women of Jerusalem

Reading

Large numbers of people followed him, including many women, who mourned and lamented for him. But Jesus turned to them and said, 'Daughters of Jerusalem, do not weep for me; weep rather for yourselves and for your children. For the days will surely come when people will say, "Happy are those who are barren, the wombs that have never borne, the breasts that

have never suckled!" Then they will begin to say to the mountains, "Fall on us!" To the hills, "Cover us!" '
(Luke 23:27–31)

Silence

Reading: Jesus Speaks to Women Today

In Mexico thousands of women work in the export factories along the border with the United States. They work twelve or more hours a day, often in unsafe conditions. Soledad works in a factory where women are forced to take pregnancy tests. If they are found to be pregnant they are fired. But, together with a local organisation, women are getting together to form health and safety committees. Here they can discuss their problems and get advice. Emilio Alvarez, who works with them, says, 'Even though we have so many problems, I really feel we're making team-work with God!'

Silence

Reading

Mexico, like other indebted countries, relies on exports to pay the interest on its debts. 'My country is like a football team made to play a very unfair game,' says Emilio Alvarez. 'Our opponents are 20ft tall while we haven't even got any football boots.'

Prayer

All:

Jesus, our friend and our brother, through your life and your journey to the Cross, your death and Resurrection, you have shown us how to live in love. May we always follow your example, living a life of compassion, in the search for peace through justice for all your people.

9 Jesus Falls the Third Time

Reading

Let me say to God my Rock,
'Why do you forget me?
Why must I walk so mournfully, oppressed by the enemy?'

Nearly breaking my bones
my oppressors insult me
as all day long they ask me,
'Where is your God?'

Why so downcast, my soul,
why do you sigh within me?
Put your hope in God; I shall praise him yet,
my saviour, my God . . .
(Psalm 42:9–11)

Silence

Reading: Today Jesus Falls the Third Time

Tracksoa Mwemba is trusting God that nothing goes wrong this year. The income from his harvest in 1997 was so low he had nothing to left to save for emergencies.

'I couldn't even buy spare parts for my plough,' says the 40-year-old farmer from Monze diocese in southern Zambia. 'If my tools break this year I'll just have to dig with my hands. And if that happens my crop will be even smaller.'

Silence

Reading

While children go hungry, only one-tenth of Zambia's arable land is being farmed and the country is importing food which poor people can't afford to buy.

Freda Luhila, director of the Programme Against Malnutrition, says, 'Zambia doesn't have money to build roads, bridges and storage facilities. But every day we find money to pay our debts.'

Prayer

All:

Jesus, our friend and our brother, through your life and your journey to the Cross, your death and Resurrection, you have shown us how to live in love. May we always follow your example, living a life of compassion, in the search for peace through justice for all your people.

10 Jesus is Stripped of His Garments

Reading

When the soldiers had finished crucifying Jesus they took his clothing and divided it into four shares, one for each soldier. His undergarment was seamless, woven in one piece from neck to hem; so they said to one another, 'Instead of tearing it, let's throw dice to decide who is to have it.'
(John 19:23–24)

Silence

Reading: Jesus is stripped of his garments today

In Bolivia there has been wave after wave of job losses. The man shining tourists' shoes . . . on La Paz's main street is Selvestre Hiladi, aged 51. He lost his job in a factory, and now feels that he has no choice, 'We old ones have to do whatever we can,' he says, 'you have to swallow your pride.'

We, the housewives, ask ourselves: What have we done to incur this foreign debt? Is it possible that our children have eaten too much? Is it possible that they have studied in the best colleges? Have our wages become too great? Together we say, no, no we have not eaten too much. No, we have not dressed any better . . . Then to whom have the benefits gone? Why are we the ones who have to pay for this debt?

Silence

Reading

More than eight out of ten Bolivians live below the poverty line. Bolivia's debt is £3.12 billion.

Prayer

All:

Jesus, our friend and our brother, through your life and your journey to the Cross, your death and Resurrection, you have shown us how to live in love. May we always follow your example, living a life of compassion, in the search for peace through justice for all your people.

11 Jesus is Nailed to the Cross

Reading

When they reached the place called The Skull, they crucified him there and the two criminals also, one on the right, the other on the left. Jesus said, 'Father, forgive them; they do not know what they are doing.'
(Luke 22:33–34)

Silence

Reading: Jesus is Nailed to the Cross Today

Matilda Makombe and her husband are both working, but she says, 'Economic Structural Adjustment Programmes, called

ESAPs for short, are designed to cut public spending so that Zimbabwe can keep up its debt repayments. But it means that the cost of basic groceries has gone up from £11 to £55 a month. It's really harsh for me and my husband, but when you think of a family with children you can't imagine how they are surviving. Some families survive with just one meal a day. That's why the ESAPs are known as the Extended Suffering of the African People.'

Silence

Reading

Nearly half the population of Zimbabwe does not have the money to buy enough food for their daily needs.

Prayer

All:

Jesus, our friend and our brother, through your life and your journey to the Cross, your death and Resurrection, you have shown us how to live in love. May we always follow your example, living a life of compassion, in the search for peace through justice for all your people.

12 Jesus Dies on the Cross

Reading

When the sixth hour came there was darkness over the whole land until the ninth hour. And at the ninth hour Jesus called out in a loud voice, 'Eloi, Eloi, lama sabachthani?' which means, 'My God, my God, why have you deserted me?' ... Then Jesus gave a loud cry and breathed his last.
(Mark 15:33–34, 37)

Silence

Reading

When I met 16-year-old Marjerie, despite sitting upright, her short breath betrayed her very poor health. She had hours to live. In all likelihood, she was suffering from an opportunistic AIDS infection, probably TB. Marjerie died shortly after I met her. Her parents buried her along with two other children.

Silence

Reading

Zambia spends three times as much paying interest on its debts to rich countries as it spends on health care. AIDS sufferers elsewhere in the world have access to medicines that can increase their quality of life, and prolong it. But these medicines are far too expensive for people who only earn £20 a month, like most Zambians. 'No hospital can afford the medicines, no family can afford them,' says Joe Chilaizya, a Zambian journalist. 'So the doctor is effectively telling them, go home and die.'

Prayer

All:

Jesus, our friend and our brother, through your life and your journey to the Cross, your death and Resurrection, you have shown us how to live in love. May we always follow your example, living a life of compassion, in the search for peace through justice for all your people.

13 Jesus Is Taken Down from the Cross

Reading

Joseph of Arimathaea . . . asked Pilate to let him remove the body of Jesus. Pilate gave permission so they came and took it away. Nicodemus came as well . . . and he brought a mixture of myrrh and aloes, weighing about a hundred pounds. They took the body of Jesus and wrapped it with the spices in linen cloths.

(John 19:18–19)

Silence

Reading: Jesus is Taken Down from the Cross Today

Benita Louis is 14 years old and lives with her family on a small farm in . . . southern Haiti. She has just been given four fruit trees by a Haitian environmental organisation . . . She says, 'I was really excited when I was told about the project. We were told about the importance of trees to our environment . . . In three years' time I will sell the fruit in our local market and pay for my education out of the money I earn. These trees will not only help us with our school fees. They will send an important message to other children and our parents that trees are important . . . Now if I see someone cutting down a tree, I tell them that their actions affect all of us.'

Silence

Reading

Income per person per year in Haiti is £79. This is the lowest in Latin America.

Prayer

All:

Jesus, our friend and our brother, through your life and your journey to the Cross, your death and Resurrection, you have shown us how to live in love. May we always follow your example, living a life of compassion, in the search for peace through justice for all your people.

14 Jesus is Buried

Reading

Pilate granted the corpse to Joseph who bought a shroud, took Jesus down from the cross, wrapped him in the shroud and laid him in a tomb which had been hewn out of the rock. He then rolled a stone against the entrance to the tomb. Mary of Magdala and Mary the mother of Joset were watching and took note of where he was laid.
(Mark 15:45–47)

Silence

Reading

David Gwemani is a Justice and Peace volunteer in his diocese in Zambia. He explains, 'I make home visits. I explain that I'm checking on the impact of the structural adjustment, which was introduced to make sure Zambia could pay interest on its debt. We ask how many in the family, who is working, if the children go to school. We ask them how they make ends meet. It causes them anxiety. Some families are not working and children not going to school because there's no money. We ask what happens when they're sick.'

'We were supposed to ask about the food basket but we've found it very difficult to do that when they're telling you their story. They sometimes say they haven't eaten for two days and they are relying on the charity of their neighbours. Most people are barely existing, they're not living. They don't even know when the next meal will come.'

Silence

Reading

Every Zambian owes creditors in rich countries three times their annual salary.

Prayer

All:

Jesus, our friend and our brother, through your life and your journey to the Cross, your death and Resurrection, you have shown us how to live in love. May we always follow your example, living a life of compassion, in the search for peace through justice for all your people.

15 Christ is Risen!

Reading

On the first day of the week, at the first sign of dawn, the women went to the tomb with the spices they had prepared. They found that the stone had been rolled away from the tomb, but on entering discovered that the body of the Lord Jesus was not there. As they stood there not knowing what to think, two men in brilliant clothes suddenly appeared at their side. Terrified, the women lowered their eyes. But the two men said to them, 'Why look among the dead for someone who is alive? He is not here; he has risen.'
(Luke 24:1–8)

Silence

Reading: Jesus is Risen Today!

In Ethiopia Mumasufiam has joined her school's food club, 'I like working in the garden,' she says. 'I'm growing peas, cabbages, potatoes and tomatoes. We tell the other children in school about the use of vegetables, how to grow and cook them and why they're important. My mother and father are very happy about the new things I am learning. We understand now that vegetables help our health and make our bodies strong.'

Silence

Reading

Debt campaigns have been launched in Europe, Africa and Latin America. Hundreds of thousands of people support the call for change.

Mulima Kufekisa from Zambia speaks out, 'What sort of economic justice is it, where those who can afford the least are expected to give to those who already have the most? Enough is enough. It's time for justice.'

Prayer

All:

Jesus our friend and our brother, through your life and your journey to the Cross, your death and Resurrection, you have showed us how to live in love. May we always follow your example, living a life of compassion, in the search for peace through justice for all your people.

Linda Jones/CAFOD
England

Fourth Station of the Cross
Jesus Meets His Blessed Mother

Stumbling down the road, through the crowds, one face stood out – His mother. Their eyes met and through her silent tears He felt the compassion she shared with Him. The joy of meeting overshadowed by the impending doom.

'My Son, why have they done this to you, you who came among us to bring hope for our future. You suffered physical pain and humiliation for them and yet they cannot see the degradation they cause is against themselves.

There will be other Mothers like me, treading their own personal Via Dolorosa; standing and watching whilst their sons give their lives to help humanity. Like me the torment of their anguish will be public, denied the dignity of bearing their grief within the privacy of their own home.

Jesus, grant them the comfort and peace of your love and enable them to accept their sorrow as a true sign of faith.'

Pat Durrant
England

Part Three

Holy Week

Into the Depths

. . . having loved his own who were in the world,
he loved them to the end. (John 13:1)

Palm Sunday
In Triumph and Sorrow

*'Hosanna! Blessed is he who comes in the name
of the Lord.' (Mark 11:9)*

A Litany of Triumph and Sorrow

For two voices or two groups

One: He comes in triumph, to a city where people are
gathered in festival.

Two: He comes to challenge power and vested interests, to
overturn status and wealth.

**Come, Christ, in triumph and sorrow,
Hosanna in the name of the living God.**

One: He comes in celebration with a royal welcome,
declaring God's reign of love.

Two: He comes to rejection, to the fearful and proud who
sacrifice him to preserve their power.

**Come, Christ, in triumph and sorrow,
Hosanna in the name of the living God.**

One: He comes to acclamation, to people waving and
shouting praises, a procession of joy.

Two: He comes to abuse, to shouts of crucifixion, false trial
and the way of the cross.

**Come, Christ, in triumph and sorrow,
Hosanna in the name of the living God.**

*Jan Berry
England*

Upon a Donkey's Back

Upon a donkey's back, the king of love rode by,
there was no turning back,
whatever they might cry.
The prophet's dream, the promised king
for whom they sing, comes to redeem.

The people thronged about, threw clothing in his way;
'Hosanna Lord', they shout
and palms before him lay.
How could they know that he had come,
God's only Son, to be laid low?

Into Jerusalem to face the power of sin,
the child of Bethlehem
for humankind rode in,
knowing that he the cross must face,
must take his place for you and me.

How easy it would be to turn and run away,
but how would people see
the living Lord today;
If he had fled and had not died,
been crucified, rose from the dead.

Now Lord alive today, remind us that you dared
to ride upon that way
because for us you cared;
So help us too, turn dark to light
And wrong to right, as you would do.

Tune: Croft's 136th or Darwall's 148th

Colin Ferguson
England

Palm Sunday

I wonder, Jesus, what you saw as you rode the donkey into Jerusalem on that day of triumph. Surely you saw the crowd you had wept over as you contemplated its lostness and malaise. It was an anonymous, undifferentiated crowd, fickle and easily led. Very easily could a person lose a sense of self and identity to drown in the crowd's anonymity. They wanted you to multiply the loaves always, to restore the ancient empire of David and Solomon and to vindicate the religion of Israel surrounded by a hostile culture. You had a different vision, a vision of a Reign of reconciliation, love, holiness and justice. The crowd's vision was myopic and its desires easily manipulated. The effusive Hosanna hymn became a clamour for blood and crucifixion. Help us to know our deepest desire, the God you are, the God who slakes our thirst and satisfies our hungers. Help us to say our Yes to the deep desire of our hearts to seek only you and your justice.
Amen

Frank Regan
England/Peru

A Very Special Occasion

In Kenya whenever an important person visited a local area this was a very special occasion. The people would cut large banana leaves and stick them into the ground to make a long processional route for the VIP to travel through. Also, they waved fronds of grass and branches of trees as the person passed. This was always accompanied by singing and dancing. Very similar to Palm Sunday in Jerusalem.

Peter Grimshaw
England/Kenya

Donkey Theology

A young man from Papua New Guinea in conversation with two elders in Jamaica

Mr Cunningham, an elder, said, 'Patient man ride donkey.' To ride a donkey is not a joy-ride because the first lesson to learn is patience. If a rider is impatient and wants to reach his destination quickly by forcing the donkey, he will eventually find himself struggling against the donkey. Often the donkey comes to a halt or moves slowly. Patience is one of the virtues you learn from bearing with the hesitant behaviour of the donkey.

Another elder, Mr Morris, liked to point out how humbly a donkey carries its load. He owned a donkey and knew how useful donkeys were as a means of transportation. They carry water, cane, people, they pull carts and travel long distances as well. They help with farm work, carry food for individuals and families. Donkeys know about weight. Mr Morris quoted Mark 8:34: 'Then Christ called his disciples and said "If anyone wants to come with me, he must forget himself and carry his cross and follow me." In Jamaica, a donkey often carries two hampers placed on the right and left of its back. It is like a yoke, a burden to carry. The donkey is the symbol of the cross.'

Koloma Make
Papua New Guinea

Song of the Palms

This could be learned by a group of children and recited as they wave palm branches with appropriate movements. If you make the palms from green tissue paper, they will rustle appropriately with the movement, but another group using suitable percussion instruments could also accompany this. The rest of the congregation could have word copies (or put on OHP) and join in each verse as it is repeated for a second time.

Waving gently
Watching, whispering
The King comes riding
riding on a donkey
He is coming
He is coming

Waving wildly
Singing, shouting
Praise to the King
Hosanna, hosanna
He is here
He is here

Waving wistfully
Watching, wondering
what will happen
to the King in Jerusalem
He is going
He is going

Heather Johnston
Scotland

Star Cross

In the star we see the cross;
Its points, the thorns,
The azure ring, his robe.
The light which shines on all
The arms which embrace all.

And this despite their mockery,
Mock majesty, pageant pantomime and pomp.
All human conceptions of kingship
Border on the Vaudeville
Verge on the burlesque.

Kings in a stable
Out of proportion
Distorted, like the body on the cross.
Our attempt to nail down Divinity
Racked and disjointed,
Still suffering our mock homage.

Cast crowns, cast lots, cast off your
Tawdry kind of kingship –
So much dressing up –
Christ rides triumphant over cast-down cloaks
Every inch a king with none of the apparel.

His crown, the star
The cross, his throne where he
Invests the cosmos with his gift of Love, unadorned.

Laurentia Johns OSB
Stanbrook Abbey
England

Hope and Solidarity

Lord, you set your face towards Jerusalem and walked along-side those who suffer. Be our vision that we too may walk the way of the cross and extend a hand to those we meet.

Lord, give us the gladness of your help
And support us with a willing spirit.

Lord, you stopped to heal the sick, cure the lame and give sight to the blind. Be our vision that we too may give time to others and respond to their needs.

Lord, give us the gladness of your help
And support us with a willing spirit.

Lord, you said, 'The first shall be last and the last first.' Be our vision that we too may work towards your kingdom when the exalted will be brought low and the lowly exalted.

Lord, give us the gladness of your help
And support us with a willing spirit.

Lord, you ate with tax collectors and sinners and heard their stories. Be our vision that we too may listen to the despised and rejected and value their lives.

Lord, give us the gladness of your help
And support us with a willing spirit.

Lord, you took time to pray and time to be silent. Be our vision that through our prayers, fasting and almsgiving we too may draw closer to you and find your way.

Lord, give us the gladness of your help
And support us with a willing spirit.

Lord, you entered Jerusalem with peace in your heart. Be our vision that we too may desire peace where others desire war, and may work for justice where injustice reigns.

Lord, give us the gladness of your help
And support us with a willing spirit
For you are our hope and our salvation.

Annabel Shilson-Thomas
England

Violence

vile	ion	nil	cove
viol	voile	lion	Levin
vole	line	clone	lee
love	lie	con	level
clove	vine	lone	lo
Clive	vice	cone	ice
Vi	voice	one	in
live	eel	oven	on
eve	Nile	coven	no
Eve	nice	cloven	I

This could be given to the gathered community for reflection. Then share with a neighbour some of their thoughts. What are the connections they made in this piece of writing?

Are there links they would make with the passion story?

Pat Livingstone
England

The Clowns Come

The clowns come
And I am disturbed
White-faced clowns who terrify me.
When they fail, attempt and fail –
We are invited to laugh. But falling hurts and failures
    invite judgement
This is not a matter for laughter.

Perhaps they are a symbol of hope
Repeated trial in face of failure
But hope is not, essentially, laughter
And I am a bewildered child again.

Oh yes, the adult in me coolly discerns
Applauds an unexpected sermon
Startled from complacency
By these familiar/unfamiliar forms
Only, deep down, I am troubled by the change of face
The masks painted to emphasise chosen expression
Limb, elastic-jointed, colours unexpected, broken.

Is this setting Your face towards Jerusalem
Knowing what is to come, yet masking because we
    cannot cope with it?

Wendy White
England

Crowd Control

By and large I don't do crowds.
Too easy to get lost in one –
Forget who you are as you adopt the crowd's persona.

Echoes of the Easter story?

In cheap supermarkets people queue halfway down the shop.
Silent for the most part.
Where I come from speaking English isn't necessarily the
    most useful language there.
The poor, the marginalised, the Kosovan refugees (amongst
    others) queue here.
Word has got round that these shops are cheap.
We queue silently, patiently with some resignation.
There are never enough staff and they never stay.
Suddenly there's a shout that a new till will open.
There's ugly pushing forward.
The fastest, the fittest, the smartest
Hurl their trolley loads onto the conveyor belt.

The solidarity of patience dissolves as families push
To be first or second.
The group dynamic is lost.

Echoing those crowds, those peoples?

They herded us through a long corridor of mounted police.
To be honest I didn't realise how massive those working
    animals are.
They herded us – several hundred – into a street
And just held us.
It was hot.
We stood shoulder to shoulder,
Hemmed in by a line of great chestnut horses.
– Odd this country sight in metropolitan London.
Some of the men began singing 'YMCA'.
Laughter and good-humoured replies from the uniformed
    riders.
We stood a long time.
And finally when my claustrophobia was beginning to grip
    me,
They moved in formation
Like sluice gates lifting
And we flooded through to the tube.

Echoes?

That sense of crowd identity.
They shouted together in joy, in venom, in fear.
And once their message was vented,
They melted away
And rediscovered who they were.

Pat Livingstone
England

124

Twenty Centuries Past

Twenty centuries past, what city has not heard of your
　　coming?
From Beijing to Berlin, from Jerusalem to Johannesburg, from
　　New York to New Delhi
surely the word has spread that you've come in peace, not
　　violence
to enrich, renew, transform our lives and bring us to shalom?

**Blessed is he who comes in the name of the Lord. Hosanna
in the highest.**

Twenty centuries past, what city has not heard of your
　　church?
From Catholic, Orthodox, or Reformed, Anglican, Evangelical
　　or Pentecostal
surely the message of acceptance, healing, confidence
in your royal advent, has been passed on through faithful
　　living?

**Blessed is he who comes in the name of the Lord. Hosanna
in the highest.**

Twenty centuries past, what city has not rejected you?
From penthouse to tenement, from factory to leisure centre,
　　from theme park to concert hall,
surely the news is that this life is for taking, not giving
and what stands in the way of this lifestyle must now be
　　removed?

**Blessed is he who comes in the name of the Lord. Hosanna
in the highest.**

Twenty centuries past, what city does Christ seek to enter?
From leafy suburb to shanty town, from housing estate to
　　West-End flat, from salon to slum,

surely the sign of the church free from pride, united in deed,
must be the welcome Christ longs for as he enters your city?

Blessed is he who comes in the name of the Lord.

John Young
Scotland

We Pray for the Modern City of Jerusalem

As the crowd shouted with joy
As the Pharisees shouted in anger
As Jesus wept over Jerusalem.

We respond with shouts and groans
And words and sounds and silence . . .

We pray for the modern city of Jerusalem.

We pray for those who shout loud and who are given power
But abuse that power
And their victims.

We pray for those who cannot express themselves freely
    Because of their faith, or their mental health,
Or their sexuality, their economic or social backgrounds
    Or just because of other narrow-mindedness or prejudice.

And lastly we shout with joy for signs of hope and inspired
    visions
Perhaps from artists or poor folk,
priests or politicians.

We offer our shouts of joy and despair,
Frustration and anger,
Relief and much more to You our God.

Amen

Where there are line breaks space was left for response.

Members of the gathered community were given percussion instruments and invited to respond to the prayers using these instruments, or by voices or words/sentences as they felt appropriate.

Pat Livingstone
England

Forgive Us and Heal Us

Leader: Lord, you entered Jerusalem to cheers of 'Hosanna' and left with your cross to cries of 'Crucify'.

We remember the times we have made you in our image, the times when we have called our own aspirations yours, the times when we have misunderstood the way of the cross and have deceived ourselves and others.

Give us strength to journey with you and grace to discern the way that is yours.

Lord of the cross,

All: **Forgive us and heal us.**

Leader: Lord, you overturned the tables of the Temple money-changers. You said, 'My house shall be called a house of prayer.'

We remember the times when we have failed to make connections between our lives and our faith, the times when we have remained complacent and inert in the face of injustice and have violated your bodily temple by our selfishness and greed

Inspire us to work for justice and fill us with the desire to build an integrated community of faith.

Lord of the cross,

All: **Forgive us and heal us.**

Leader: Lord, you were anointed by an unknown woman in preparation for burial.

We remember the times when we have been too busy to love you, the times when we have failed to recognise your needs in others, the times when we have made ordinary that which is special and dismissed that which is precious.

Impassion us with the love of an unknown woman, that we may serve you in friend and stranger.

Lord of the cross,

All: **Forgive us and heal us.**

Leader: Lord, you humbly took a towel and washed the feet of your friends.

We remember the times when we have fought for prominence, the times when we have desired power and have forgotten those without a voice, the times when we have pursued our own freedom and enslaved others.

Give us courage to embrace your service freely, to take up your cross and follow you.

Lord of the cross,

All: **Forgive us and heal us.**

Leader: Lord, you knew that Peter, who called you the Christ, would deny you three times.

We remember the times when we have denied you and have been afraid to speak the truth, the times when we have followed the path of safety and have ignored the path of risk.

Empower us to change, to become the rock on which you build your Church, that we may go forth to proclaim your kingdom and build up the body of Christ.

Lord of the cross,

All: **Forgive us and heal us and make us one in heart and mind to serve you in humility. Amen**

Annabel Shilson-Thomas
England

Donkey Day

Cross-marked beast
bearing cross-burdened Christ,
what is your message today
as you travel the palm-strewn way?
Stumbling on a stony track,
people's coats on your back,
you were chosen for faithfulness.
This is a calling we share,
as the cross-marked hill
comes closer still.
Your job is to carry him today,
yesterday's weight forgotten;
tomorrow's burden still uncertain.
May we, his cross-marked people
bear him just as faithfully.

Janet Lees
England

Monday to Wednesday of
Holy Week
On a Roller Coaster

*'The Lord is near to the broken-hearted, and saves
the crushed in spirit.' (Psalm 34:18)*

Holy Week

'Holy Week'
the name we use
as if to sanitise the shame
of deep disdain,
by calling it a worthy name:
the noblest we could choose.

'Holy Week'
a ritual time
in measured steps of liturgy
of 'we urge thee . . .'
in prayers from earnest clergy
in careful, crafted rhyme.

'Holy Week'
a separateness
from smoothly spoken platitudes
and gratitudes
no room for easy attitudes
to heal this deep distress.

'Holy Week'
a watershed
where love comes face to face with fear

and hate is near
and how we turn to sin is clear
and yet for us Christ bled.

'Holy Week'
the end, the start:
the firmly planted cursed Cross
a sign of loss
the naked pain an end to gloss
in solitude apart.

'Holy Week'
the end, the start:
the Cross is bare, the tomb is void
and death destroyed
and resurrection hope deployed
for each repentant heart.

Stephen Brown
Scotland

Temple Scene

Matthew 21:12–17

With waving palms, the crowds have greeted Jesus on his triumphant entry into Jerusalem. Riding on a donkey, he enters the city, knowing full well that his arrest, trial and crucifixion are now only days away. But there is still so much to be done before his earthly ministry is fulfilled. He has only limited time left with his chosen disciples, and he knows that the temple police and teachers of the law will be looking out for ways to trip him up.

Despite that, he heads straight for the Temple – the most holy building in Jerusalem. And there he finds the traders, buying and selling, changing money for the temple offerings, and selling the sacrificial animals required by the law. What they were doing was needed, and done with the blessing of the Temple authorities – but it had got out of hand. *Mammon was taking precedence over, and getting in the way of, God. Jesus saw red, and we have the familiar passage where, for perhaps the only time in the Gospels, we see Jesus resorting to physical violence.*

He overturned the tables of the money-changers and the stools of those who sold pigeons.

I used to like that reading, Lord,
I could close my eyes and see you,
    anger spilling over into action,
Upsetting the tables,
Upsetting the status quo,
Driving the merchants from the temple.

I could see the pigeons fluttering away
    from those trying to sell them,
I could see the chaos –
Some shouting at you,
Others trying to retrieve the escaping birds,
Yet more scrabbling on the ground,
    hoping to find the coins,
    and none too concerned at whose coins they were.

I could hear you, Lord,
The anger coming through in your voice.
Calling them thieves as you pushed them out of the courtyard,
    pushed them outside into the street
Looking at those who stayed there still
    and telling them this was a house of prayer.

I could feel the heat of the sun, Lord
    beating down, that day,
    bouncing off the whitened walls of the temple
    and of the houses beyond,
Adding to the fraying tempers
    as people shouted back at you,
    and argued with each other.

The bewilderment of some,
   the anger of others,
   the confusion perhaps of the temple guardians themselves
as the normality of every day
   was turned upside down
   into a heaving, turbulent chaos.

And no one seriously able to come back at you,
   for they knew you were right.
Even as their trade went topsy-turvy,
   they knew they had no case to argue.

I liked that picture, Lord.

I liked it, perhaps because I get angry at times,
   and in my conceitedness
   I sometimes like to think
   that my anger is as justified as yours,
   that my indignation could be called righteous.

I liked it, Lord, perhaps because I felt no guilt.
Those men were wrong, Lord.
Not like us, here, now.
We don't have money changers in this church,
   no one comes here to sell pigeons
We honour your temple of prayer.

And in self-satisfied smugness,
   I dare to identify myself with you
   and condemn those you attacked.

Then, Lord, I go silent
   as I understand what caused your anger:
   the anger that came from seeing people exploiting
      their position of power:
   the one-sided bargains being made;
   the anger that came because those people were erecting
      barriers
      that hindered others entering the temple to pray.

And then I know that I am as guilty as they were.

I betray you time and again, Lord,
   for you demand honesty in every part of my life, not just on
      Sundays –
And are all my dealings so honest
   that I am not like the money changers?
Do I never try to exploit those around me
   just as those traders in the temple did?

Lord, if you were here today,
   how would you see me?

And do I still put up barriers that hinder other people coming
to You?
Do my words or my actions,
   my adherence to tradition,
   my clinging in comfort to the familiar way –
   do all these say to others:
   'This is my God – worship Him on my terms'?

Lord, if you were here today,
   how would you see me?

Lord, let me come to you now.
Drive out my smugness, my complacency,
   my self-satisfaction.
Drive out all that separates me from you,
   all that keeps others from getting close to you.

Lord, let me come to you now
In humility and seeking your forgiveness
Lord, let me come.

And I pray you will show me the mercy I do not deserve. Amen

Brian Hudson
England

Cleansing the Temple

Regarding the situation as an absolute disgrace,
Jesus enters the Temple area with ever quickening pace.
In anger He throws down the pigeon-dealers' seats
and upsets the tables of the money-changing cheats.
'My house shall be called a House of Prayer',
those within the precincts hear Him declare,
'but you are making it a bandits' cave.'
The guilty, not trying goods or coins to save,
fly in haste, not seeking to make reply,
not daring to look Lord Jesus in the eye!
After noise, confusion, bustling and escaping,
the Lord turns to those still there waiting –
some blind, or almost so and some rather lame.
They feel his healing touch and are made whole again.

Rosemary S. Watts
England

Turning the Tables

The four pieces – Caleb the Temple Trader, Daniel the Money Changer, Gaius the Gentile and Eliazar the Priest – were written to be used in a Holy Week service highlighting the incident of Jesus overturning the tables in the Temple. Worship took place in the round and the place was in a mess. Upturned tables and chairs, scattered hymn books and Bible, coins, feathers and loose papers were everywhere.

Opening worship could include the hymn 'We love the place, O God' followed by spoken prayers, followed by:

Leader:

Apart from a few comments, you've all acted as if nothing has happened here. 'It's all part of the event,' you've said to yourselves. But what if it was for real? It has happened in some churches. Why destroy and desecrate a beautiful, holy place like this? Who would do such a thing?

Then the four pieces are performed, each preceded by a different Gospel version of the story:

Mark 11:15–18 – Caleb
Matthew 21:12–13 – Daniel
Luke 19:45–46 – Gaius
John 2:13–22 – Eliazar

Hymn: 'To Bring a City to its Knees' by Andrew Pratt

Leader:

Now let us sit quietly for five minutes – a long time, if you're not used to the silence.
Look at the mess.
Reflect on the characters you have heard.
Remember that the only one to speak in favour of Jesus and to have a real longing for worship was the Gentile – an outsider, not a Jew.

Then think about the question:
How would Jesus react to what is going on in your church? Or in your life? No one will be asked to give an answer.
Just think honestly about it.

Prayers

Hymn: 'Lord We Know that We Have Failed You' by Nick Fawcett from New Start Hymns and Songs

Blessing

The following pieces can be performed together or separately as each one stands alone.

Marjorie Dobson
England

Caleb – Temple Trader

You wouldn't believe it unless you'd seen it, but the man was absolutely mad. And nobody did anything about it. They just cowered against the walls and watched. I don't know where the police were, but they certainly didn't arrive in time to do anything. It was just absolute chaos and there was nothing you could do.

I suppose it just all happened so quickly. I mean, it was only an ordinary day. There was no warning of trouble – in fact, business was very good that day. There were masses of people milling around and you would have said that the general mood was excited and cheerful, until that man turned up. Passover week is always like that. Some people come to the Temple then that may never have been in Jerusalem before – and they're always in good spirits – and ready to spend.

My stall was set up in the usual place, just a little way in on the right hand side – I always say it's no use being too near the entrance, because people go past you before they know you're there. But by the time they get to where I am, they're starting to look round and that's the time when I try to catch their eye. I've always been noted for good merchandise – you ask anyone – 'You can't get a better pair of doves than from Caleb,' they'll say. And I charge a fair price. They're not cheap, I grant you. The only way to get a cheap pair of doves is if you bring them from home. But anybody who's got as far as the Temple before they think about buying doves for sacrifice has to recognise that it will cost them more. I have to pay more for them myself – and then it's certainly not cheap to have my stall pitched in that particular part of the courtyard – the Temple authorities must be coining it in! Then there are my other overheads, my own taxes, my profit margin – well, by the time you've worked all that out, you can easily justify my prices. Everybody knows that town-centre shopping is expensive – and if you're actually trading in the Temple . . . well!

But that trading is perfectly legitimate. There was nothing wrong with what I was doing. The authorities were happy with it. It's been going on for years. And it doesn't stop people from worshipping in the inner courts of the Temple. I would have thought it was considered very convenient – having all the supplies on site, as it were – especially for those customers who live in the city itself. It was all going very well and I'd built up a very healthy business – until that maniac arrived.

He even took a whip to some people, you know! It was disgraceful. Throwing over the tables was bad enough. Two of the legs of my stall were totally smashed and as for the doves – well, I'll never see them again! But Jonathan, next door, was even worse. The end of the whip caught his cheek and I shouldn't think the scar will ever fully heal.

And that maniac, Jesus, had the nerve to be raging that it was his father's house and we'd made it a den of thieves and robbers. I don't know who his father is, but Jesus has certainly disgraced the family name.

I hope they lock him up and throw away the key – when they find him. Of course the Temple police were not around when they were needed and only turned up when the villain had disappeared. But apparently he's known as one of those wandering teachers who's built up a large following, so it shouldn't be too difficult to track him down. According to all reports, he's only been known, up to now, for miracles of healing and telling good stories – oh, and having a go at the scribes and Pharisees with a few scathing comments – but then, who doesn't? But today in the Temple he was a real wild man – maybe he's just beginning to show his true colours.

As long as they catch him, that's all that matters to me – although I wouldn't mind a bit of compensation for loss of trade. But, in the meantime, I suppose I'd better find a carpenter who can make me some new table legs. Can you recommend anybody?

Marjorie Dobson
England

Daniel – Money-changer

What the hell did that man think he was doing?

And what right had he to be there in the first place?

Can you see what he's done to my money? It's all over the place. I'll never get it all back – the thieves and vagabonds around here have already been in scavenging, and because all my records are scattered all over the place, I'll never be able to find it all.

The villains are having a field day. They came pouring in as soon as they heard about the riot and they've been stuffing their pockets ever since.

It's outrageous!

I'd never even heard much about this 'Jesus' before – except for that extraordinary story that has been going round about the reformation of Zaccheus the tax-collector.

Reformation, indeed! What did Zaccheus need to reform from?

He was a legitimate government official – going about his regular business – raking in something on the side, of course, but that's just part of the job – and good luck to him, that's what I say.

He's no different to me. We charge a legitimate rate of interest. After all, you can't buy the money you need to use in the Temple from any other source than us money-changers, and everybody has to do it. You can't use your everyday coinage here.

So we are providing a service – and the interest we charge is only to keep us in business. Every business has to make a profit, or it doesn't last long.

So what's so different about being a trader in the Temple? You have to change your money somewhere – and where better than on holy ground? It puts money in the Temple coffers, so what's so wrong about it?

That man was out of his mind. All he's done is cause chaos and mayhem and lined the pockets of a few petty thieves. And left an enormous mess for somebody to clear up.

Why should he be allowed to disturb us like this? We've been going on this way for years and nobody has been too bothered about it before. What's wrong with my business? Money dealing is my way of life and always has been.

And as for calling this Temple precinct a den of thieves and robbers . . . ! Well, it may not have been before, but it is now. Look! There's another one after my coins!

Hey! Get away out of here! The Temple's no place for such as you!

Marjorie Dobson
England

Gaius – the Gentile

I don't know who that man was, but I'm right behind everything that he did. This place has just become beyond a joke.

It's all right for the Jews themselves, they can go through all this chaos into the other courts of the Temple. Even the Jewish women are allowed to go into the next one, at least.

But for us Gentiles, this is the only part of the Temple that we *can* come into. 'The Court of the Gentiles' they call it – as if we were a separate breed from the rest of them.

But that man was right – they have made it into a den of thieves and robbers. Those money-changers are raking it in – they charge as much interest as they possibly can.

And the dove and animal sellers use the system to their own ends. They claim they are the only ones with animals pure enough to be sacrificed and they make sure that the examiners at the gate turn away any birds and animals that have been brought in from outside.

Talk about a monopoly on sales! They've got it made!

What's more, because of their exorbitant prices, even the mildest mannered people are ready to protest.

Add to that the sellers shouting their wares and the animal noises and the smells – I ask you, is this really a place of worship?

But, as Gentiles, we have no choice.

I suppose they just assume that Gentiles don't really come to worship – only to look at the sights.

Well, most do, I suppose. Especially at a time like the Passover when there's a lot going on and people are in a celebratory mood. The Jews certainly know how to party.

And there's something about their religion that intrigues me. After all, as a race they've had a lot of setbacks, but they still cling to this idea of only one God and one that will always see them through.

That's what keeps drawing me back to the Temple. I'm curious to know whether their God would accept me – and I'd love to find a quiet place here, where I could ask a question or two and sit and reflect. Maybe even pray.

There's been no chance of that recently and I don't think the Jews even considered how we Gentiles must have felt. They're too busy trading and arguing and trying to do each other down.

I wouldn't care so much, if it wasn't for the fact that they claim to be such religious people.

But there's no reverence here and not a chance of finding God. I'm sure they don't even realise how much their behaviour puts people off. After all, if you can't talk to God in their principal place of worship, where else are you going to find him?

But that seems to be their last consideration.

Maybe that man who charged in here and upset everything has some answers?

He was certainly very, very angry and was determined to make his point.

What's more, he seemed to have his priorities right and he was saying just what I felt. You'd have almost thought he was speaking for us Gentiles – which is very unusual for a Jew.

I'd like to see him given a chance to sort the place out properly, because he seemed to mean business and wasn't afraid of anybody.

Good for him, I say. I just hope it doesn't get him into too much trouble, but knowing the Temple authorities, I doubt if they'll let the matter lie.

But I hope he's shaken them up a bit – they certainly need to be.

Marjorie Dobson
England

Eliazar – the Priest

This is the last straw. We cannot let this go on any longer.
We've let it go too far already.

We have watched this man wandering round the country-side, gathering his crowds and teaching and claiming to heal.

We've seen plenty like that before and usually they can be left to their own devices and contained within their own area – as long as we know what's going on.

But this Jesus always had a dangerous air about him – even as a young boy.

Apparently he was able to debate with the teachers here in the Temple and hold his own against them. There are one or two of our older colleagues who remember him clearly and say that he had a remarkable mind and was mature for his age.

After that incident we heard nothing from him for nearly twenty years – until he started his wandering ministry after being baptised by that wild prophet, John.

We started to smell a rat when he showed he was quite capable of giving clever answers to some of our trickiest questions.

He also began to be very subversive about some of our rules and regulations – claiming scriptural backing for his healing on the Sabbath and quoting King David when he was caught out eating ears of corn in the field – on the Sabbath again.

Then he started to speak out directly against us – warning people not to take too much notice of our outward piety – as if we were standing on street corners praying just to show off to the people!

A little publicity for the faith surely doesn't do any harm – and someone's got to do it.

But he called us hypocrites – two-faced – and insisted that our hearts weren't in our religion. He said people should look at our behaviour and judge for themselves – implying that we were saying one thing and doing another.

Who is he to judge?

But we've been insulted before. We're used to it – and we ignore most of it.

Nobody can be perfect – although we don't tell the people that, of course – we have to set them standards to live up to – and nobody knows what goes on behind our closed doors.

But what right has anyone to criticise us?

They don't know the responsibilities and strains of leadership – especially with people as volatile as ours – even with their so-called faith in God.

These last few weeks though, this Jesus has become dangerous.

We knew from our informants that he was determined to come to Jerusalem for the Passover and the combination of him and his followers and the Passover pilgrims was not a prospect to be savoured.

Then there came that procession into the city!

Now that really did set the alarm bells ringing. The crowd might not have realised the significance of him riding on a donkey, but we did.

He was setting the battle lines. This was a real challenge to our authority.

I still would not have thought that he would have the nerve to do what he did today.

We couldn't bar him from the Temple – it was his right to make a sacrifice.

We just kept an eye on him.

But nobody anticipated what he was going to do next – not even his followers.

He just seemed to suddenly blaze with anger and then stormed around with that whip, destroying everything and declaring it to be 'his father's house', not a den of robbers.

That 'father's house' claim cannot be tolerated.

It's another step on the road to him claiming to be the Messiah and it must end – before people really start believing him.

It's time for real action – but this time, on our part.

He must not be allowed to continue!

Marjorie Dobson
England

A Surprising Fragrance

Such extravagance,
it seemed,
to Judas watching
Jesus' anointing.
And we, Good God,
might say the same:
as if the symbol cost so much
that could be better spent:
bruised and bent reeds
healed, not just unbroken.

And yet, O Lord,
some times must be
when we anoint the ordinary
with eternity:
symbols said and symbols done:
mountainous righteousness,
cosmic love,
kingly servanthood,
fragrant death.

And so, Loving God,
we call this week 'holy'
not to say all others are profane

but to help our faith find focus
in the passion of the Cross;
where symbolic words met crude reality
in rustic, ritual death:
with the fragrance, surprisingly, of love.

Stephen Brown
Scotland

Jesus the Carpenter

Jesus the carpenter, hanging on Calvary,
nails through your feet and your work-hardened hands –
wood you have worked with and wood is your destiny –
paying the price of our sinful demands.

You came to our world as a part of a family,
living and learning the carpenter's trade.
You followed your father's instructions so faithfully,
shaping and crafting the yokes that you made:

Jesus the carpenter . . .

You called other workmen to join in your ministry,
laying rough hands on the sick and the lame.
You taught of God's love with such power and authority,
People who knew you believed you insane:

Jesus the carpenter . . .

You faced with great courage the open hostility
coming from those who believed they were right.
They stripped you and beat you and laughed at you finally,
thinking your death was the end of the fight:

Jesus the carpenter . . .

But we, who now know that you ended triumphantly
working with wood till your task was complete,
can come to your cross with our hope and humility,
laying our pride at the Carpenter's feet:

Jesus the carpenter . . .

Marjorie Dobson
England

Betrayed!

Betrayed! The 'Jerusalem one',
innocent of all charges,
and Judas is our scapegoat.
   Forgive us, Lord,
   for with Peter, we deny
   and with Judas we betray.
   Deep fear compromises love,
   and we separate ourselves
   in unholy disjunction
   from truth.

And the silence of shame
overwhelms us.
And the sorrow of tainted silver marks us.
   Forgive us, Lord,
   that privileged though we are
   to know the drama's full tale,
   we sell faith cheaply,
   and seek smooth phrases of excuse.

*Stephen Brown
Scotland*

Washing One's Hands

Washing one's hands of the conflict
between the powerful and the powerless
means to side with the powerful,
not to be neutral.

Paulo Freire
Brazil

Love Unknown

This was written as a visual prayer with the appropriate tools and wooden objects being used. The congregation is asked to keep their eyes open.

Love unknown, Lord, how could you do it?
Coming from the glory of the Father to a carpenter's workshop in Nazareth?
Taking on the ordinary, the everyday, the working life?

And yet, in choosing the life of a carpenter, you chose well.

Carpenters working with wood can shape it and cut it down to size and make it right for its purpose.

Carpenters can smooth rough edges and make joints that dovetail and shave off the corners of square pegs so that they can fit into round holes.

And in their spare time they can work with the wood and the grain to make objects of pleasure and beauty – even including the flaws.

Carpentry was the right choice for you.

Jesus the Carpenter, take us in hand and shape us.
Plane our rough edges, transform our faults and flaws and make us fit for your purpose.

Work on us, Lord, and help us to work with you, so that what we create together will be strong and useful.

And when we face the crosses we all must bear in life – knowing, as you did, that there is nothing we can do to change the situation – let us remember your strong workman's hands were useless against the nails – but you faced it and went through it.

Christ the Carpenter, we draw our strength from you.

Marjorie Dobson
England

Spirited Dancer, a Pantomime Figure

To Jesus who leads the way to freedom through the world's derision and a cross.

Spirited dancer, a pantomime figure,
comic, distorted, misused and abused;
never expedient, working with rigour,
seemingly foolish yet never confused.

Crying the wilderness down on your shoulders,
offering pedants the cool time of day;
I would dance with you, by paths or rough boulders,
willing to enter the fun or the fray.

Now in my cowardice, my fear, apprehension;
sharing the life that you've given to me;
help me to put away pride and pretension,
learn in your footsteps the way to be free.

11.10.11.10 metre

Andrew Pratt
England

Peter

Hello! My name is Peter – yes, that Peter!

The one who said, 'I will follow you anywhere, Jesus.' The one who was so full of himself when he recognised that Jesus was the Christ when nobody else seemed to. The one who was so proud when Jesus recognised him as a tower of strength and called him 'the Rock'. The one who set out to fight off the soldiers when Jesus was arrested. The one who denied even knowing Jesus when trapped by that young serving girl in the courtyard.

I'm that Peter. Not much to be proud of there, is there?

But I was different then.

I didn't have a bad start in life really. People think of fishermen as always being poor, but our family owned its own boats and you had to have a certain knowledge of business to succeed with so much competition around. And I was working with my brother, which made it a lot easier. Andrew and I are a bit like chalk and cheese, but that didn't do us any harm really. I was always prepared to take more of a risk – and he held me back if he thought I was doing anything really dangerous. We rubbed along together well enough and looked out for each other – and the great thing about Andrew is that he is very generous to those he cares about – and not just with money.

That was how I got to meet Jesus in the first place.

Andrew came rushing in all excited one day and told me that I must meet this very special teacher he had been talking to – and Andrew is not the kind of person who gets that excited unless there is something really special in the air. So, I went with him and, as you must know by now, that was the start of the biggest adventure of our whole lives. We were so thrilled by it all that we just left everything – family, friends, even the boats – and it's only afterwards that we realised how much of a shock that must have been for our father. But we weren't the only ones – and we did go back into the area occasionally – remember the time when Jesus healed my mother-in-law?

Life with Jesus was amazing! You never knew what would

happen next. His teaching was different from the rest of them – and he really spoke as if he knew what he was talking about – not as if he'd just studied it to qualify as a teacher. The numbers of people who came to him for healing were overwhelming, yet he always dealt with as many of them as he could. He had a marvellous fund of stories – even if we didn't see the point of them all straightaway! And he certainly got the crowds on his side when he started on the Pharisees and Sadducees and the scribes – especially when he told them exactly what he thought of them – and even accused them of being hypocrites!

But that was also when the warning bells started ringing and we realised that he was putting himself in real danger, so we tried to *redirect* him a little – not that he took any notice of us!

Yet we had some strange experiences with him too.

The strangest was at the top of that mountain – where we saw all that glowing light and those two men, who appeared to be Moses and Elijah. We hadn't a clue what to do, so I opened my big mouth again and suggested that we should build special places for them to stay – one of my dafter suggestions, I have to admit!

I don't think any of us understood what was going on with Jesus there, but we noticed that he started talking more about his death after that – almost as if that strange experience had been some kind of confirmation. I tried once to stop him talking about death and going to Jerusalem and he practically bit my head off and called me Satan, so I knew I'd put my foot in it again.

I kept doing that kind of thing, swearing allegiance one minute and letting him down the next, but the biggest mistake I made was the one I thought that I would never be able to put right.

We were all so tense in those last days with Jesus. I wouldn't say that we knew he was going to his death – we didn't – not really. He'd said he was, but we were so full of his ministry and the fact that the crowds always seemed to be on his side – and we just didn't see the danger signals.

And *none* of us could see what was happening inside Judas.

Even to this day I can't understand his behaviour. He seemed to be as big a follower as any of us. But we were all different anyhow, so we didn't realise that he'd gone off on his own way and had been dealing with the enemy behind our backs.

But I have no right to be judgemental about him – not after what I did.

After all, I had been the one who protested when the soldiers came to arrest Jesus. I'd always been used to defending myself and I wasn't going to let them take Jesus if I could help it. It was the wrong thing to do, of course – or at least Jesus said it was – so I had to let him go without any more protest. But I was going to try to keep him in sight if I could. That was why I followed to the High Priest's courtyard and pushed my way to the fire – so that I could be near the action.

Unfortunately I didn't understand how the mood of the crowd was changing once Jesus was in enemy hands – and I just didn't think how dangerous it would be for me to be in that place. Andrew wasn't there to hold me back, I suppose.

It was only when that servant girl looked at me in that strange way and then asked me directly whether I was a friend of Jesus that I looked around and saw just how many hostile faces there were. So I panicked, didn't I? And I couldn't believe I was hearing myself denying that I knew Jesus. But once I'd said it I couldn't go back.

They seemed to ignore me for a bit after that, so I hung around, but then I must have said a few words to somebody about how cold it was and they recognised my northern accent and started on me again.

I was *really* frightened that time and my tongue got the better of me, as usual, and I found myself cursing and swearing that I didn't know this Jesus in any way.

Then I heard the cock crow – three times – and immediately I was back with the memory of Jesus telling me, only the night before, that I would deny him three times. I was devastated, because suddenly Jesus was looking at me and I knew that he knew what I'd done – even if he hadn't actually heard the words I'd said. I didn't know what to do with myself and I just wept and wept and then I ran away.

The next days are a blur. I knew they were crucifying Jesus, but I couldn't go anywhere near – I couldn't bear the sight.

But the most difficult thing to deal with was the fact that I'd betrayed him and I was never going to get the opportunity to say how sorry I was. What could I do to put it right? It was all over. Finished! Done! And I'd messed it all up – again!

They told me that Judas had committed suicide and I think I was the only one who felt any sympathy for him at that time. He'd been a betrayer, but then so had I. If I hadn't had family responsibilities to go back to I might have followed the same route myself. And when the women started talking about the fact that Jesus had come alive again I just didn't believe them – you don't get a second chance with life.

When they finally convinced me that it was true, it didn't make me feel any better – in fact I was terrified of facing him again, because he knew exactly what I'd done – even if I'd managed to hide it from the others. So I kept such a low profile that they wondered what was wrong with me. Which is why I escaped to the lakeside, the one place that I have always found I could get some peace.

Jesus knew where I was. Of course he did. And I didn't know where to put myself when he came towards me.

But then he asked me if I loved him! The answer was 'Yes', but how could he believe me after what I'd done? Three times I told him that I did – at first hesitantly, but then with more confidence – and then I suddenly realised what he was doing – he was forgiving me.

And he was giving me a new start – telling me to look after people in his name! He knew I'd learnt my lesson the hardest possible way – *and* he knew I wanted a chance to start again.

You know the rest!

We didn't really take off in our work until the Holy Spirit came that Pentecost, but then things were never the same. All of us found hidden depths in ourselves and we were just as it had always been with Jesus – never knowing what was round the next corner, but always pushing on to new challenges and new opportunities.

A chance to start again after real failure – that's what Jesus gave me and that was the message I took with me wherever I went.

Jesus had always been in the business of changing lives and starting again – I should have realised that it applied to me as well!

Marjorie Dobson
England

God of Hope

God of hope we ask you
To clothe us in compassion
And enfold us in your love.

Send us out with the joy of Christ
To feed the hungry with good things.

Send us out in the peace of Christ
To prepare a banquet for all peoples.

For you will lift the pall of death
And banish our sorrow.
You will wipe away our tears
And we will dance with joy.
Send us out
There *will* be no more mourning
Send us out
There *will* be no more pain.

God of hope, we hear you
God of life, we will answer your call.

Linda Jones
England/CAFOD

Dying and Rising

'Unless a grain of wheat falls into the earth and dies, it remains just a single grain; but if it dies it bears much fruit.' (John 12:24)

These powerfully awesome words weave through the events of Holy Week. They reach a climax in the crucifixion. Jesus dies in order that life may be celebrated. His compassion for the many folk with whom he spoke and to whom he listened propels him towards Calvary. His love for those who were marginalised by the religiously respectable within his own tradition undermined order and security, as well as the standing and power of which they were very defensive. This verse is about life, not death. Life in all its fullness is the passion of Jesus. He could not refuse to know, love, touch and respect people who were powerless and whose spirit was being choked by religious dogmatism and fear. The dying leads to a flourishing. The person and ministry of Jesus could not be held in check by death. His death is the extent of his passion for people; the proof of that passion lies in the miracle of resurrection.

Holy God, help me to recognise those things to which I must die,
the mere routine of church life,
the prejudice that lies unspoken and yet shouting within me,
the carelessness with which I read your Word in the scriptures,
the habits which crowd out spontaneity,
the fear of listening too closely to my neighbour.

Holy, God, you created life, you created me for life,
You offer life to be lived with celebration,
with joy and with love
for the sharing of your kingdom
for the speaking of your justice
and in gratitude for your grace.

Help me to live for, with and in you
freely, willingly and delightfully
reaching for the passion of Jesus.

John Ll Humphreys
Wales/Scotland

Maundy Thursday
Broken Bread . . . Broken Body

*'This is my body given for you . . .
this is my blood poured out for you.' (Luke 22:19, 20)*

The Watershed

The garden tears are real, dear Lord, we know:
no pre-prepared rehearsed set-piece.
Your brow creased tight with sweat like blood,
we see you suffering agonies.

The dark shroud of the night-time a sign
of greater dark and harsher pain to come,
but still you set your will against yourself
and drink the bitter cup.

And we who eat and drink
in sacramental wonder
connected by bread and wine
in close communion defying time,
gather in that upper room:
and find you stooping to wash us.
The watershed.
Despite our pre-prepared
rehearsed set-piece of table talk,
still searching words puncture complacence:
'If I do not wash you,
you have no part in me.'
The watershed.

And then to watch and wait in prayer,
arrest is near, the scent of death in the air.

Stephen Brown
Scotland

Maundy Thursday

Six women, Jesus, wait on you,
Not expectant, not waiting for a miracle,
Not believing you will leap to life before us and cause the
    blind to see,
But simply waiting;
Being with you, being God.

No men have stayed – too busy,
Called to this and that activity –
This waiting business is women's work:
But Jesus waited,
Being holy, being God.

He waited for the woman with the haemorrhage to pour
    out her story;
He waited for Lazarus to be dead before calling him from
    his tomb;
He waited for Judas to lead his enemies to him;
He waited for the verdict of the people: Crucify!
He waited on the cross while his life blood left him,
Waiting in faith, in control of his death.
He waits now for us to turn towards him.
Longing for us to know he is waiting.

And so, here we are, we women who wait;
And as we wait we listen.

Sarah Ingle
England

There in a Garden

There in a garden when God called my name
I could not face him because of my shame
Trust I had broken, I ate from his tree
God forgive Adam for Adam is me.

There in a garden Christ knelt down in prayer
I helped them find him and I led him there
They took and killed him on Calvary tree
God forgive Judas for Judas is me.

There in a courtyard as Jesus was tried
I do not know him – three times I replied
There as the cock crowed was my treachery
God forgive Peter for Peter is me.

There in a garden he rose from his tomb
When we were hiding he entered the room
Doubt not my living my wounds you can see
God forgive Thomas for Thomas is me.

Now in my life, Lord, in my everyday
I need your guidance to show me the way
Faithless and fearful no more let me be
Be my forgiveness and come alive in me.

Colin Ferguson
England

Jesus in the Garden Weeping

Jesus in the garden weeping,
on the ground disciples sleeping,
through the night the soldiers creeping –
Judas leading all the way.

Jesus, his accusers facing,
Peter in the courtyard pacing,
full of fear, his heart is racing –
in his weakness, he'll betray.

Jesus on the cross now dying,
at his feet his mother crying,
John, alone, his help supplying –
in the shadows women pray.

Jesus in the garden risen,
proving death was not his prison.
Mary saw the angel vision –
'Do not seek him here today.'

Jesus in that room appearing
to his friends, their spirits cheering.
'Peace be with you,' in their hearing
drove their guilty fear away.

Jesus, when we are mistaken,
when our hold on faith is shaken,
grant forgiveness, Lord, awaken
us to Easter hope this day.

Tune: 'Quem Pastores', 8.8.8.7 metre

Marjorie Dobson
England

A Woman Walked to the Altar

In a rural church in South Africa the minister had travelled a long distance to conduct the communion service. He discovered that he had brought the wine but forgotten the bread. The nearest town was at least 20 miles away and the shops closed until Monday morning. The session leaders sat and debated the problem while the congregation continued to sing hymns. An old woman suggested, 'Let us tell the people', but this idea was considered too radical. Finally, after 45 minutes and unable to find another solution, they decided to tell the congregation what the problem was. When the minister made the announcement a woman walked to the altar and offered some bread. She had brought it to feed her children after the service.

Andrew Prasad
India

Let's Go to the Maize Field

Let's go to the maize field, the maize field of the Lord.
Jesus Christ invites us to his harvest of love.
The maize crop shines in the light of the sun,
let's go to the maize field of communion.

The people press forward crowding round the altar,
snugly round the fires the whole congregation
gathers here today.

Communion's not a mythical, vain and empty rite.
It's a commitment to live by.
It's getting the point of Christianity.
It's joining in the struggle of everyone together.

It means saying, 'I'm a Christian and so therefore,
  brother and sister,
You can sing with me.'

Harvest Communion Song
Central America

An Easter Sonnet: Paschal Lamb

Death passes over the blood of the lamb
smeared on door posts and lintels,
each year follows a pattern and plan
shaped by ancient rituals.
The chosen one kneels in humility
a towel tied round his waist,
washing away the dust of the city
from his followers' feet.

He breaks the bread with a blessing
offering, feeding, sustaining;
he shares the wine with thanksgiving
pouring, spilling, saving.

This last meal that they are sharing
is our first meal of remembering.

Heather Johnston
Scotland

Sharing the Meal

Lord, we give thanks as we share the meal
Which links our hearts with thoughts of you;
As we remember the words you spoke
We can know you make all things new.

Sharing the bread we are one with you,
Your wine of life restores our soul;
Living and learning within your love
Means the broken can be made whole.

Lord, as you blessed the disciples' food
And turned the water into wine,
Transform our lives by the holy bread
And the fruit from your living vine.

Cecily Taylor
England

When Jesus Shared

When Jesus shared his bread and wine
and faced his final day –
Did we not promise, we will stay?

When Jesus in Gethsemane
asked us to watch and pray –
Did we not sleep the night away?

When Judas kissed him on the cheek
and soldiers took our Lord to slay –
Did we not also run away?

When Jesus was reviled and mocked
and we were asked to own his name –
Did we not also love betray?

When Jesus walked towards his cross
and stumbled on the way –
Were we not hidden far away?

Colin Ferguson
England

Eat of the Christ Bread

Taste the bitter herbs of passover and eat to make us fit;
fit to travel across an unknown desert's sand;
fit to seek a promised land
where humankind and God shall fully live,
for God does love and does forgive
those who really share his feast.

Eat of the Christ bread, for what we eat is broken heart
    and soul,
hung on a cross because of love's great need
to heal the sick, to help the hungry feed,
to free, give hope, to let all people live,
for God does love and does forgive
those who really share his feast.

Drink of the Christ wine, for what we drink is blood and
    tears,
tears shed for those who die alone,
blood shed when people will not own
the life and hope he freely gives,
for God does love and does forgive
those who really share his feast.

Feed on the Christ food, for what we taste is life in all its
    fullness,
life wholly given, life that is meant to share,
life spent and bent in service and in prayer,
life consumed in everything we give
to God who loves and does forgive
those who really share his feast.

Colin Ferguson
England

Guilty, Or Not Guilty?

For Holy Week/Maundy Thursday

This piece is best performed in the round, so that everyone can focus on the table (a low one is best), which is centrally placed and contains a cross, a clear glass bowl, a clear jug of clean water and a towel.

It is ideally done with five different voices, but can be performed with less, if the roles are doubled up. The speakers should be dispersed around the circle, except for the two who perform the last piece – they should sit together.

The order of readers is Pilate, Neighbour, Critic and Not Us!

When Pilate has finished speaking the second reader from Not Us moves forward to the table, pours the water from the jug into the bowl and takes it and the towel over to Pilate, who washes his hands (no soap) and dries them. The bowl and towel are placed back on the table. When the Neighbour has finished speaking, it is Pilate who offers the bowl. For the Critic, it is the Neighbour and for the Not Us couple it is the Critic. This way each speaker is linked to the guilt and this is really why it is better with five people.

When the last couple have finished speaking and washed their hands, the bowl is placed on the table. It will be seen that the water has changed colour. After a pause for reflection the leader of worship moves forward and lifts the bowl so that all can see it. Then these words can be used, or the leader can respond with personal reflections on what has happened.

We have listened to what these people have had to say about themselves and, no doubt, in our own minds we have made judgements about them. Guilty, or not guilty! Each of them came here with clean hands and, because they were able to justify themselves in their own eyes, they washed their hands free of guilt.

Their hands were clean, but the water is now dirty. What does that mean?

And what would happen if we each washed our hands in the same water? We know that it would only deepen the colour. Are our hands ever really clean?

It may not be appropriate for every group, but perhaps after a period of silent reflection some people from the group may also wish to wash their hands in the bowl, as a sign of penitence.

The worship would end most appropriately with reflective music, or 'When I survey the wondrous cross', sung quietly.

Marjorie Dobson
England

Pilate

I was uneasy about this whole case from the start. Nothing was right about it and the Jews are such devious people to deal with – well, their leaders are anyway – and they have their own means of getting the crowd on their side.

It was inevitable that something like this would happen here. My friends warned me when I was given the job, but once I was appointed I couldn't very well refuse, could I?

But I was warned that the Jewish religion was a tricky one to handle and I know to my cost that it's true.

So when they brought this wandering teacher in, it was bound to mean trouble. If the Sadducees and the Pharisees and the High Priest were all already against him, then what chance did he have?

The charges they brought against him didn't seem to mean a great deal. They said he claimed to be a king – which was supposed to put me on my guard in defence of the Emperor – but Jesus said himself that he wasn't intending to be that kind of a king and then started talking about other worlds and heaven. That seemed quite harmless to me – deluded, but harmless.

But somewhere in the middle of my questioning I was sent an urgent message from my wife, warning me to have nothing to do with the case. Now this really did make me feel uneasy. She doesn't normally have any interest at all in my official hearings – she knows it's none of her business – so this was very different.

Apparently she'd had a frightening dream about this man, Jesus – and she'd been so alarmed that she'd taken it very seriously.

I would have ignored it, but I was struck by the note of fear in her message. She is unhappy here, I know. She misses her family and friends and her social life. No-one here has taken on Roman ways, except Herod, and he hadn't made us feel welcome at all. So I've been used to her complaints about everything and her constant wish to get back to real civilisation – but I've never known her to be so agitated about one of my cases with a particular Jew before. Perhaps she realised that in this case I held the power of life and death, although it's not the first time. Maybe her servants had been pleading for the man. He seems very popular with such people. But whatever the source of the message, it slightly alarmed me and made me anxious to get the case off my hands.

It was then that somebody mentioned that Jesus was a Galilean and I thought I had the answer. Send him to Herod! He was in Jerusalem – let him deal with it. The priests and the lawyers wouldn't be happy about it, but they had no choice, and I thought that would be the last I would see of them that day.

Herod didn't do anything at all! I shouldn't have expected that he would. All he ever wanted was to be entertained and to keep himself out of harm's way. But he didn't get the entertainment, because Jesus didn't speak a word, so Herod dressed him up for his own amusement and then sent him back to me.

We talked it over later that day – Herod and I – and we knew we'd both been manipulated, but what could we have done? That was the first time that I realised that he and I might be able to get on with each other after all.

But his attitude didn't solve my problem. The priests and lawyers were still baying for the Galilean's blood and by now they had stirred the crowd up, so that they were also demanding his crucifixion. I did have one more trick up my sleeve. The Jews' own custom was to have a prisoner of their choice released at the Feast of the Passover and I thought I might just be able to persuade them to release Jesus. I was only half right. They did want Jesus released, but not my prisoner. It was another Jesus they were shouting for – Bar Abbas, Jesus Bar Abbas – a notorious villain if ever there was one. If there were those in the crowd who were shouting for Jesus of Nazareth, their cries were being twisted to sound like something else, or drowned out altogether.

I tried – I really tried to persuade that crowd – but it wasn't a crowd, by this time it was a mob. And they wanted blood. The blood of Jesus the Galilean.

In the end I gave in. There would have been a riot otherwise and many innocent people would have been hurt, or killed.

So Jesus became a sacrifice – and the strange thing was – he didn't fight it!

But I will not take the blame upon myself. I tried hard to do something about it, but I was overwhelmed by circumstances. They were to blame – and the priests and the lawyers and the ones in the crowd who were really against him. They stirred up that uncontrollable mob, not me!

Which is why I took the basin and the towel and – where everyone could see – I washed my hands of the whole case.

My wife was pleased, but I can't forget what I have done – it haunts me. I can't wash his blood from my hands with water. I wish there was some way that I could.

Marjorie Dobson
England

Neighbour

Based on a true case

You'd never believe it if I told you what my neighbours do to their children. I don't think they're being deliberately cruel, you understand. But, it's just . . .

Well, I know they both work very hard. They have to, to keep body and soul together. They already had the little girl when they moved in next door and you could tell they didn't have much money when you saw the few tatty bits and pieces of furniture they brought with them. It wasn't very long after that when I saw she was pregnant again – she may have worn loose clothes, but I could tell why she was doing it. She carried on working though, so did he. He was on nights; she worked days in the local shop. They must have hardly seen each other – in fact, it makes you wonder how . . . well, never mind!

Then, when she had the new baby, she lost her job and was at home all the time. In fact, that was when I first starting speaking to her – when I saw her coming past my door with the baby in her arms and the little girl trailing behind. Well, you have to say something about a new baby, don't you?

We spoke once or twice after that. In fact, I was beginning to think she was quite nice, until that day she told me she'd got a new job. I was pleased for her – until she told me it would mean her working nights as well as her husband.

'What are you going to do about the children?' I asked her.

'Oh, they'll be all right!' she said, 'the baby sleeps right through and I'll make sure the little girl can't wander out of the bedroom until I get back.'

I just stared at her, 'What do you mean?'

'Well, I've got one of those strap things you use to keep hold of a child when you're out with them. You know, one end fastens to their wrist and the other to yours. I'll just fasten one end on her wrist and the other to the bed, then she'll be safe.' Just then the baby started crying and off she went.

And that's what they're doing. I see them go off each night – she goes first, he goes an hour later and she gets back about two in the morning. I hear her coming up the street and opening and shutting the door. And all I can think of is those poor kids left on their own – one of them tied to the bed.

But what can I do? It's none of my business! My friend says I should report them to the NSPCC, but I can't do that. They would know who it was that had done it. And I'm not offering to look after the kids either – that's their problem, not mine. Surely they've got some family or friends – let them sort it out.

I really do think something ought to be done. But it's nothing to do with me!

Marjorie Dobson
England

Critic

Pauses should be made between each complaint

Isn't it disgraceful how people these days don't seem to care about the church any more? The only time you hear them saying the names of God and Christ, they're using them as swear words. And some people have never seen the inside of a church unless they've been to a wedding or a funeral – and most of them don't take place in church any more.

I blame the schools. When we were at school we were taught all about the Bible and Jesus – even if some of the teachers weren't very good at it. But we were taught to sing hymns and to learn the Ten Commandments and how to say the Lord's Prayer – and they don't get that kind of thing in schools today.

And we were sent to Sunday School as well. I remember we had to learn a verse from the Bible every week, and if we could remember it we got a sticker with a Bible picture on it. There was always a competition to see who got the most.

Most children these days don't even come to Sunday School – or Junior Church, or whatever new-fangled name they call it. Some of them go to Scouts, or Guides, or one of those things, but they evidently don't teach them much about church there either. You can tell that by the way they behave on the odd occasion they do turn up for special services. But you can't get the right people to run these things – not even the Sunday School. Nobody seems to want to make any kind of commitment. They can't do – they're always appealing for more people to help out.

But the parents don't help at all. Young parents these days always seem to have so much to do. Going to church isn't one of their priorities – oh, no! They're far more likely to be at the supermarket, or watching football, or taking the children out for the day. They don't seem to want to give their children any lasting values. Everything has to be bright and new and entertaining. They can't see how much comfort there is in doing things in the old-fashioned ways.

The minister doesn't help either. Always trotting off to do school assemblies and charity meetings and sending other people to visit instead of coming himself. He should be concentrating more on his preaching – some of the ministers in my younger days used to draw crowds of folk to church to listen. It doesn't happen very often now.

But there's nothing I can do about it. It's not my fault if people don't want to know. I've lived a good life, as far as I can, and as long as the church lasts out for my life-time, that's all that matters.

Marjorie Dobson
England

Not Us!

Details in these pieces can be changed, as appropriate.

Voice One: We inherited the problem –
Voice Two: – said the National Coal Board when it took over the coal tips at Aberfan.
Voice One: It's all a matter of economics –
Voice Two: – say the multi-national companies destroying the rain forests.
Voice One: It's political and part of our history –
Voice Two: – say warring factions all over the globe.
Voice One: We don't make people buy –
Voice Two: – say the drug barons.
Voice One: We don't expect people to do this in real life –
Voice Two: – say the makers of violent or pornographic films.

Pause

Voice One:	We're giving people what they want –
Voice Two:	– say the brewers – to the family of an alcoholic.
Voice One:	We're giving people what they want –
Voice Two:	– say the tobacco firms – to a victim of lung cancer.
Voice One:	We're giving people what they want –
Voice Two:	– say the Lottery organizers – to the family of a mother who never has enough money for food.
Voice One:	We're giving people what they want –
Voice Two:	– say the credit card companies – to the families who are never out of debt.
Together:	It's not our problem!

Marjorie Dobson
England

Truth and Subversion

Jesus is brought before Pilate: John 18:28–40

Narrator:	Early in the morning Jesus was taken from Caiaphas' house to the governor's palace. The Jewish authorities did not go inside the palace, for they wanted to keep themselves ritually clean, in order to be able to eat the Passover meal. So Pilate went outside to them:
Pilate:	What do you accuse this man of?
Priest:	We would not have brought him to you if he had not committed a crime.
Pilate:	Then you yourselves take him and try him according to your own law.
Person One:	We are not allowed to put anyone to death.
	Pause
Narrator:	Pilate went back into the palace and called Jesus.
Pilate:	Are you the King of the Jews?

Narrator:	Jesus answered.
Jesus:	Does this question come from you or have others told you about me?
Pilate:	Do you think I am a Jew? It was your own people and the chief priests who handed you over to me. What have you done?
Jesus:	My kingdom does not belong to this world; if my kingdom belonged to this world, my followers would fight to keep me from being handed over to the Jewish authorities. No, my kingdom does not belong here!
Pilate:	Are you a king, then?

Pause

Jesus:	You say that I am a king. I was born and came into the world for this one purpose, to speak about the truth. Whoever belongs to the truth listens to me.
Pilate:	(Slowly) And what is truth?

Pause

Narrator:	Then Pilate went back outside to the people.
Pilate:	I cannot find any reason to condemn him. But according to the custom you have, I always set free a prisoner for you during the Passover. Do you want me to set free for you the King of the Jews?
Person One:	No, not him!
Person Two:	We want Barabbas!
Narrator:	(Slowly) Barabbas was a bandit . . .

John Davies
England

This dramatic reading can be followed by discussion and the prayer below, 'Deliver Us and Give Us Peace'.

Deliver Us and Give Us Peace

Lord Jesus
by your cross and resurrection	**deliver us**
by your witness to the truth	**deliver us**
by your passion and death	**deliver us**
by your victory over the grave	**deliver us**
from the lust of power	**deliver us**
from the conspiracy of silence	**deliver us**
from the worship of weapons	**deliver us**
from the slaughter of the innocents	**deliver us**
from the nightmare of hunger	**deliver us**
from the peace that is no peace	**deliver us**
from security that is no security	**deliver us**
from the politics of terror	**deliver us**
from the plundering of the earth's resources	**deliver us**
from the dispossession of the poor	**deliver us**
from the despair of this age	**deliver us**
by the light of the gospel	**give us peace**
by the good news for the poor	**give us peace**
by your healing of our wounds	**give us peace**
by faith in your word	**give us peace**
by hunger and thirst for justice	**give us peace**
by the coming of your kingdom	**give us peace**

Amen

John Davies
England

Wash Hands – Be Clean?

Not mine the hands that fashioned
Cluster bombs providing jobs
In some suburban park

                                        'Yet it is one

Not mine the fingers keying codes
Of laser-guided death on helpless
Cowering conscripts

                                        of you who dips

Not mine the fear or hate that spills
A nation's blood and anvil-hammers
Ploughs to pangas

                                        a hand in

Not mine the empty bowl held high
In trembling hand that pleads enough
For just another day

                                        the dish with me

Not mine the stocks and shares, or power,
The throne, the mitre or the Mace
To sway a different destiny

                                        who will betray me'

Edgar Ruddock
England

Jesus Took Off His Robe

One of the most remarkable moments during the Last Supper sees Jesus strip off his robe and stand naked before his disciples in order to wash their feet. This poem-sermon – whose form perhaps allows for a more concentrated use of language and imagery than is usual in a sermon – attempts to explore the significance of that moment.

The rustic rabbi thus removes his robe –
the presser of flesh exposes now his own
tired torso, stripping dignity quite bare –
the first of many exposes of flesh
on this, a night for torment, lashings sore –

for now, Love's hands caress the watered feet
to strip away accumulated grime.
Encounter – flesh on flesh – more deeply points
to nakedness where vulnerability's shown.

The first embarrassed, glancing lovers' touch
perhaps elicits lack of letting go,
a slight but fearsome freezing of the heart,
a holding back – this risk's too much to dare.
But if love's true the nervousness will pass
through passion which is intimate and deep,
awakening dependency long sought,
a confidence to go beyond the flesh:
deceit unmask, the soul unburden, trust,
to cleanse each other's hurt – redemption find.
Reversing paradisial precedent.

When Eve and Adam, sensing that their God
would come, uncovering sin just newly made,
stripped leaves from off life's tree to cover guilt
exposing follies further – as God flung
them far towards a future, barkless tree,
a leafless, listless, Golgothean Rood,

whereon hangs naked flesh, stripped real and raw,
the hands of love compressed by sealing nails,
a burdened God, his body sunk with sin
to heal that first and very human fault.

Tonight the church is stripped, as we expose
uncluttered stone, undecorated wood.
Our feet are washed, our open hands receive
his fragile flesh, his whole self freely given.
Will we our hands soon wash, avert our gaze
and implicate ourselves in Pilate's haste?
Or will we cast off layers deep within,
unveil the truth and with Christ freedom win?

*This poem-sermon was preached at the Cathedral Mass on Maundy Thursday, 20
April 2000, at St George's Cathedral, Cape Town. It is based on John 13:4 –
previously preached at the Parish Mass on Maundy Thursday, 1 April 1999, at
St John's Church, Friern Barnet, London, UK.*

Chris Chivers
South Africa/England

I Heard of a Child . . .

I heard of a child
    and the child was painting
        and the painting was a face
           and the face was crying
and the tears were the colour of blood.

I heard of a man
    and the man was praying
        he was praying in a garden
           and he was sweating
and the sweat was the colour of blood.

Gerald O'Mahony SJ
England

You Know Me, Lord

Who? Me?
You must be joking!
Whatever the rest do
I'll always stand by you –
You know me, Lord.

Who? Me?
I didn't fall asleep,
maybe the others did
but I just closed my eyes –
You know me, Lord.

Who? Me?
With Jesus?
Of course I wasn't
You've made a
  mistake
I don't know him.

Who? Me?
I've told you
I don't know
  the man
never met him
never knew him.

Who? Me?
Sound different?
I'm not from
  Galilee
never been there
don't know what
  you mean.

and the cock crowed!

Who? Me?
You still want me?
Even though I denied
I ever knew you?
But then –
You know me, Lord.

Yes. I know you.
That's why
I want you
to tell others
that you know me.

Heather Johnston
Scotland

A Heroic Prayer

I would rather
  be here with you
  than anywhere else
  without you

I would rather
  have nothing
  and be with you
  than have everything else
  without you

I would rather be mocked and ridiculed
  with you
  than be living comfortably
  and well thought of
  but without you

I would rather hold to your truth
  and take the consequences
  than live an easy lie.

I would rather have you for my King,
  crown of thorns and all,
  than follow any other leader.
Remember me.

Gerald O'Mahony
England

Good Friday
The Most Harrowing Time

'My God, my God, why have you deserted me?' (Psalm 23:1)

Simon of Cyrene

The crowd was restless,
waiting,
murmuring to one another.
In the distance women were wailing.
A voice cried out,
'He is coming',
Roman spears glinted
through a gap among the heads
and polished shields gleamed
in the morning sun.
'There he is!' a voice cried,
and the crowd began to shout abuse,
even those who knew it was a lie,
scared to say they knew him.
They headed in my way,
forcing the crowds aside
to jeer and jostle in their wake.
Suddenly they were in front of me
and he stumbled,
the rough wood splintering down his back,
raking into his previous wounds.
I stretched out my hand
but he fell, his body worldly weak.
The soldiers cursed him, lashed him,
hauled him to his broken feet,
then saw he could not bear the load.
They seized me and gave me the cross

to carry in his place
up to the hill's accursed crest.
Ahead of me he stumbled on,
each movement full of pain
at the venom of those
who scorned his battered frame,
mocking, swearing,
though some began to pray.
I walked as if trapped in a spell,
caught in a living nightmare,
a parody of myself,
both onlooker and participant.
On we climbed,
his shame becoming mine,
but as we reached our destination
I felt that he had known me all the time
and he had borne the deepest bruises,
the cruellest pain, and our betrayal
with the fondest of embraces
and the greatest love of all.

Colin Ferguson
England

A Meditation for Good Friday

What is so good about Good Friday? On this day,
against the first warm sunlight of the spring,
the Church with perverse constancy recalls
rejection, suffering, pain, untimely death
– the cold dark winter of our human time.

Good is not quickly seen where young men die
and mothers mourn and all the sky is black
with human woe. Here in our brokenness
God too is broken: pierced through hands and feet,
bleeding and suffering with us, goodness dies.

179

Through the long day and night it lies entombed
sealed in despair's impenetrable vault
till in the darkest agony of loss
an angel's word – 'Not here among the dead,
but with the living is the one you seek.'

Love lives again – hope springs, faith breaks the stone,
seeks out the ones who, sleepless, grieve alone,
and like a well-loved friend that speaks our name,
touches our broken heart with broken hands
and turns Good Friday's pain to Easter joy.

Heather Pencavel
England

Carry this Cross

A Meditation for Good Friday

Why me?
Why pick on me to carry this cross?
I suppose I look strong, I'm used to working out in the fields
but even for a strong man, this cross is rough and heavy
I'll have a sore back in the morning
nothing like as bad as his though – stumbling along in front
   of me
his fine white robe is striped with red from the bleeding
   wounds
he doesn't look like a criminal or a troublemaker
but then, you don't need to be, you only need to upset the
   Romans
that's why I didn't argue when they said 'Carry this cross'.

We're nearly there, I can see a mound with two crosses on
he's fallen! I almost trip over him
the soldiers haul him to his feet, drag him to the mound
he stands head bowed
blood and sweat dripping from a thorny crown.

As they drag the cross from my back, he lifts his head
'Thank you', he says
his eyes looking into mine reflect pain and suffering
that is somehow more than his own
as though he is suffering the pain
of all the people in the world,
including mine, and I know
that I am willing to carry this cross
not just today, but for the rest of my life.

Heather Johnston
Scotland

Nightmare

A Meditation for Good Friday

O GOD!
How terrible it is to think that you are dead!
All our hope and vision,
all the incentive to love instead of hate,
all the light of our life snuffed out.
When we look at the world without you
we are shocked by its cruelty.
Even so we try
    to love where there is rejection,
    to make peace where there is conflict,
    to bring hope to those who despair,
    to heal where the world is wounded.
But we are bruised and beaten;
powerlessly we wait for death
and we watch those we love die without your comfort.
People blame us for being silent
and curse us when we speak.
    Without you, nothing makes sense,
        there is no reason to love,
            no reason to hope,
                to live.

But you are God!
The desolate, the sinner, the grieving, the suffering, the poor,
	the whole world needs you
		to make life meaningful, worthwhile, forgiving and
			accepting.

Only you can take away our fears by your love;
only you make sense of life.

It is easy to believe
that Good Friday is the end;
but that is a nightmare.

It is today that God in Christ takes our place.
Today is the day he dies for us.
This is the day that the Lord has made.

Colin Ferguson
England

Good Friday

What's good about it?

Outside Jerusalem
On a hill called Calvary
Three wooden crosses
Filled with pain and misery.

Then God himself
Turned out the light
Mourning for his only son
The day was blacker than night.

The world stood still and waited
'It is finished,' he cried
Bowed his head in obedience
And died.

What's good about it?
He is good.

Heather Johnston
Scotland

A Simple Wooden Cross

During the 1980s, civil war claimed the lives of 70,000 people in El Salvador. If the victim was a member of a Christian community, the members would commemorate them by making a simple wooden cross and decorating it with pictures symbolic of their life and concerns.

Source unknown

Dying with Dignity

Samraksha is an organisation in Bangalore, south India which cares for people living with HIV/AIDS. Many of the people suffer terrible deaths. A devoted group of professional women and men are working themselves to the limits as they care for people in the rapidly increasing numbers of people affected. On one occasion the director, a fine, resourceful and resilient Indian professional lady, found a man collapsed in a corridor, crumpled and dying. She took him up, cradled him in her arms and took him to a bed. A short while afterwards he died. This supreme act of care and compassion enabled this unknown man to die with dignity.

Geoffrey Duncan
South India/England

Prayers for Good Friday

Today God
we remember your pain
a crown of thorns
public disgrace
nails hammered through living flesh
blood streaming from open wounds
lungs starved of air
slow agony as life drains away

at the foot of the cross
we weep for the pain we cannot stop
and cannot bear

we weep for the victims of violence
for the innocent who suffer
from war and famine and disease

we weep for the victims of injustice
for the homeless and hopeless ones
who wander the streets and sleep in shop doorways

we weep for the victims of economic forces
for the ones who have no work and no money
and have lost their self-respect

we weep for the lonely isolated people
who are the targets of other people's prejudice
and are defenceless in the face of taunts and mockery

we weep for our own pain . . .

at the foot of the cross
we weep for the pain we cannot stop
and cannot bear.

You have borne it, Lord, you bear it with us
and your love is stronger than all our pain
stronger even than death.

We thank you for the love that bears the cross
and enters into death willingly for humankind;
for your love that lives and grows in the world by
    your spirit
in all who reach out to tend the wounds of others.

We thank you for the love that comes to us when we
    are in pain
and other people's hands reach out
to soothe the hurt and calm our fear.

We thank you for the courage of those who take up the
    pain of their people
and spend their time, their energy and their health
in working for justice and peace in politics and public
    life.

We thank you for the months and years of patient
    negotiation
and courageous persistence in the face of terrorism
which have been spent in the pursuit of peace in
    Northern Ireland
and we pray today for further faith and courage
in both leaders and people
until the wounds of the past are healed.

We thank you that everywhere in your world
the light of love shines in the darkness
from an empty cross, and cannot be put out.

At the foot of the cross
we weep for the pain we cannot stop
and cannot bear
and yet we know

that you have borne it, Lord, you bear it with us
and your love is stronger than all our pain
stronger even than death.

We give you thanks and praise
in the name of Jesus Christ, your Son
Amen.

Heather Pencavel
England

A Prayer for Good Friday

We come here today to remember a special, but tragic, day in
our Christian calendar.
On this day we look at the cross, not just as a symbol of our
faith but also as an instrument of torture and death.

Today is a solemn, sobering day, Lord – a very black day in
the calendar of the events of your life.

On this day we remember that you reaped the rewards of
being controversial in your attitude to religious bigotry.

On this day we see the betrayal of friendship and its
consequences.

On this day we remember that your enemies appear to have
got the upper hand.

On this day we remember that all the prophecies about your
end were justified.

On this day we see the casual cruelty of Roman authority and
execution.

On this day we see how unreliable your followers proved to
be in a real crisis.

On this day we appeared to see the death of God.

Be with us, Lord, as we reflect on this day and the effect that it has on our lives.

Help us to remember that religious bigotry, cruelty and unreliability are still a part of our everyday lives and that enemies of the faith still surround us.

Show us how we can learn from your example of suffering that you were prepared to go to any lengths to prove just how much God cares about his people.

Then help us to translate all that we learn into loving actions and reactions to the people around us who need that sacrificial love.

Otherwise your cross would have been in vain.

Marjorie Dobson
England

Good Friday Prayers

Holy God on this dark day we bring before you the darkest places of our world, and of our lives, holding in our souls the knowledge that even in those darkest places the cross is ever present, the place of pain, to share pain, to carry pain, to transform pain into healing.

We bring before you the dark places in our world – the places of war, bloodshed and violence where humans seek to destroy one another for power. We bring before you the places of famine where those with plenty are unwilling to share with the hungry. We bring before you the places of hopelessness – in refugee camps, on the streets, in lonely old age. We bring your cross to these dark places.

We pray for the children of the world, remembering especially those who cry with hunger, those children who cry because they have lost home and family, those children who have learnt not to cry from fear of reprisal, or because there is no-one to listen. We bring your cross to these dark places.

We pray for those who live in the darkness of pain and suffering, especially those who are ill but don't know why, those who are grieving without relief, those whose minds are in turmoil, those who are dying and are afraid, those whose bitterness at past suffering blocks their healing. We bring your cross to these dark places.

We pray for those who have died, those for whom your cross has been a stepping stone to new life. Grant us with them true faith in the power of your cross.

Sarah Ingle
England

Cross Makers

Into his hands he took an axe
and felled a living tree.
He stripped its bark and smelled its blood:
the sap of Calvary.

Into his hands he took the tree;
two heavy planks he sawed.
Rough hewn he shaped them, top and tail;
carpenter of the Lord.

To beam, and boom he took his tape,
the width of outstretched hands.
And in the centre carved a notch
to hold the Son of man.

With hammer blows on iron nails
Not once a strike he missed.
And, rising, dirty from his work,
The finished cross he kissed.

Instrumental music

And still today we crucify
our Lord, but not with planks,
but radar-guided missiles
and armour-plated tanks.

In factories across the land
cross-makers we employ,
who shape today's weapons of death;
new Christs to crucify.

Will God forgive us cross makers?
Do we know what they do?
Not 'til we banish cross and mine,
The risen Lord we choose.

Ed Cox
England

Easter People

Good Friday dawns so bright and clear, as it would have done
    in Our Lord's time,
I wonder what He was thinking as He made that final climb?
We have prayed the Stations around the Church and shared
    His painful hours,
We weep for the Man who was perfect, as His blood for us
    outpours.

Would we have been like Simon, who helped with the Cross
    on the way?

189

Or would we have been like so many are now?
'It does not concern us,' they say.
Would we have wiped His poor face with a cloth
    just like Veronica did?
Would we have helped Him get to His feet
    as under His burden He slid?

Would we have tossed for the robe He was wearing
or grabbed for a souvenir?
Or cowardly turned our eyes away, pretending that
    we were not there.
On Saturday night we wait for Him, it is the least that we can
    do,
Tomorrow we will hear He is risen and pray one day we will
    share that too.

Jean Sherriff
England

Sacrifice

The mildest suffering was the mockery
by raucous Romans with their royal robes
and cruel crown of thorns
pressed into the skull.
He did that for me.

Then there was the whip
with knotted nuggets of metal meshed into the thongs
tearing the tender flesh
when hurled by a heavy hand.
He did that for me.

And the nails
piercing, pointing, penetrating
and hammered down hard to make sure they held.
He did that for me.

And the cross
and the hanging from his hands
and the scorching sun
adding the final insult to his injury.
It doesn't bear thinking about!
I seldom do!

What do I do for him?
Suffer a twinge of conscience
as I cast my reluctant coins on the collection plate
and sit in solemn silence in a Sunday Service.

Marjorie Dobson
England

Light

Three crosses crudely caught the light
from soldiers' spears
and sore refractions from the tears
of weeping women standing silently in sight
of three young men
for whom for all they lived was lost –
their loves, their lives' hopes crossed
crossed out by Caesar's men of might.
The midday sky foreshadowed night.
One cursed and cried
and cursed the Son of God and died
completely lost. The other saw with bloodied sight
a face – the Host! –
heard lips that promised Paradise!
His curses changed to cries:
Remember me! – And there was Light!

Harry Wiggett
South Africa

Gift of a Cross

Forgive me, Lord.
Sometimes I can't quite fathom
Why you just can't make
Your eternal truths
A little easier to see.
If only Your offering to us, Lord,
Had come gift wrapped
On that dark Calvary day,
In sparkling paper
With rainbow coloured bows, perhaps,
Instead of the cruel and painful nakedness
Of fresh drawn, still warm, blood
Dripping onto rough hewn wood
Beneath a dark, forbidding sky.

If only You'd packaged it differently, Lord,
Given us the anticipation
Of reaching out
To a gift held forth in love;
Perhaps then, yes then,
We might more easily have seen
Beyond the splinters and the thorns,
Perceived
Within the wounds and through the blood
That this was not mere horrible injustice,
Jesus' death.
No, more,
Far more than that.

Holding the image of a cross
Within my mind now
I see a sinless human, precious friend,
Giving up
His very life for me,
For me and for humanity;

Focusing all the agony and pain that we might ever know
On Him.
There's comfort, Lord, in that:
To know
The man of sorrows
Understands.

But help me to see the joy within that image, Lord,
To see beyond
The starkness of the crucifixion pain,
Hidden inside
This blood-stained snapshot in eternal time,
Help me to see
The wonder
Of Your freely given
Gift.

That of a cross,

Gift wrapped

In unimaginable love.

Pat Marsh
England

For Three Hours

And for three long hours
the midday sun was blotted out
and all
was utter darkness.

I wonder,
did it all go totally quiet,
onlookers struck speechless,
birds unusually silent in the trees?

Was all in perfect stillness,
without sound,
but for the shallow laboured breathing of the Christ,
the gentle weeping beneath his cross,
the in-drawn breath
of those who watched in shock?

Was there a whispered sense of hushed expectancy,
of inexplicable awe?

Or was there a silence born from fear
and fuelled by the cold that gripped the scene
when the sun no longer shone?

Or maybe hysteria, panic, random shouting
at the spectacular blackening of the sky?

Did those onlookers even faintly understand,
remotely begin to comprehend,
the unique significance of those three hours,
three long dark hours,
in eternal time?

Do we
still fail

to fully
understand?

Pat Marsh
England

Jesus Dies on the Cross

Jesus is dying,
hanging on that cross,
upheld not by the cruel nails
but by his own great love
for all humanity.
He is brother to all who suffer,
friend to every victim.
He is one with the tortured,
with the lonely
with refugees
and all who are afraid.

Anthea Dove
England

Crown of Thorns

A 'crown of thorns'?

I had not thought of it that way.
Thorns, yes,
I'm very familiar with those;
Painful, wounding,
Nagging in the side of my consciousness;
Causing deeper wounds the more I fight the suffering.

Thorns, yes;
But a crown?

Deep wounds of suffering
Batter and bruise my heart.
Deep incisions
Cutting across all concepts of a Loving God;
Returning me again and again to
Why?
Why God, why?

In the infinity of God's wisdom
I am so small
And there seems no answer I can comprehend.

Yet the response to suffering
Has been a deep experience
Of love, courage, strength, compassion
And, dare I say it, even joy.
An intimate revealing
Of God's power to love, transform and heal.
Yes, a 'crowning' of His glory.

A 'crown of thorns'.
I see it now with new perspective.
What privilege to share that crown:
A special place and joy that none can know
Unless they've also walked the path,
The path that means
That only those who've worn the crown
Can see the crown on others.

Pat Marsh
England

Condemned Christ

Condemned Christ,
hanging in agony,
sharing the death of criminals,
we pray for those who wait:
    those who wait in pain,
    those who wait in anger,
    those who wait in sorrow,
    those who wait without hope.
We pray for ourselves,
wanting an end to pain, anger and sorrow;

aching for a new hope.
May your lingering Spirit
be the source of our life
as we witness to you
sharing pain, anger, sorrow and hope
however we can.

Janet Lees
England

The Centurion and the Soldier: 'Am I Forgiven?'

Centurion sitting at a table – tankard/mug in front of him –
enter soldier

Soldier	You all right sir.
Centurion	Eh? Oh it's you, Marcus. Sit down, though I'm not much company tonight I'm afraid.
S	Nasty business that crucifixion today.
C	Yes.
S	Pardon my saying, sir, but it seemed to affect you quite badly.
C	Yes. It did.
S	I'd have thought an old hand at executions like you would be immune by now.
C	Yes, but this one was different.
S	What, you mean the darkness and that story about the temple curtain being split in two?
C	No. That's not really what I meant. It was . . . Him.
S	You mean Jesus?
C	Yes.
S	Look sir, pardon me for saying this, but you ought to be more careful, you know, about what you say.

C	You mean, when I said that he really was the Son of God? Well, I meant what I said.
S	Sshh! You don't know who might be listening.
C	Did you hear what he said to that thief on the cross?
S	No. But I heard the thief say something about the fact that he deserved his punishment.
C	Did he deserve it?
S	'Course he did. Caught red-handed, he was stealing a sheep.
C	It was a *dead* sheep.
S	Yes, but it was also one of Pilate's collection of rare breeds taken from his private hillside.
C	I suppose nobody thought that he had a wife and seven children at home, and he couldn't afford enough food after paying his taxes.
S	Sir! You're beginning to sound like . . . Him.
C	If only I could.
S	Sir. Watch what you say or you'll find that the next crucifixion you attend will be your own.
C	If I could be sure of one thing then I wouldn't care.
S	What's that?
C	It's what he said to that thief.
S	Well, what did he say?
C	He said that he would be with him that night in paradise. That meant he was forgiven. How can I be sure that he has forgiven me?

Heather Johnston
Scotland

Surprised by Truth

*When the centurion who was standing there saw how he died, he
said, 'Truly this man was a son of God.'*

It was not where I expected a revelation.
A hot day and dirty work,
the troops restless, making feeble jokes.
Women weeping, beginning their wake.
Passers-by moving quickly
never looking at us in the eye.

The orders made it all the harder,
special attention for this prisoner,
priests watching every step,
clear up the site by sundown.

So we did the job as ordered,
usual procedure, done by the book.
But at the end, the strangest thing,
a look from him, a certain dignity,
a cry to heaven drawn out in pain
yet still a certain dignity
and a quiet resolution.
At that moment I knew he challenged me
and I said, 'Yes.'

*Bernard Thorogood
Australia*

Lord, by Your Cross and Resurrection

My God, My God, why have you deserted me?
Matt 27:47/Mark 15:34

Suffering, alone,
You, Lord, penetrated the depths of human pain.
Now through the darkest valleys of our sorrows
Our God walks with us.

> **Lord, by your cross and resurrection,
> you have set us free.**

**Father, forgive them for they do not know what they are
doing.**
(Luke 23:34)

Your forgiveness,
encompassing, embracing, lies beyond our comprehension.
Protect us from the bitterness of the older brother
who resents your generosity.

> **Lord, by your cross and resurrection,
> you have set us free.**

Indeed, I promise you today you will be with me in paradise.
(Luke 23:43)

Your heaven
You offered to a criminal, punished and rejected.
We shall gain paradise when we, like him, can recognise the
face of God.

> **Lord, by your cross and resurrection,
> you have set us free.**

Father, into your hands, I commit my spirit.
(Luke 23:46)

Daddy, you called,
take me home.
Give me the faith of the child who lies back
in the parent's arms,
certain of love.

> **Lord, by your cross and resurrection,
> you have set us free.**

Woman, this is your son. This is your mother.
(John 19:26)

Watching, she weeps
at the torture we witness.
Yet in his pain the Son offers comfort,
consolation out of the depths.

> **Lord, by your cross and resurrection,
> you have set us free.**

I am thirsty.
(John 19:28)

Our incarnate God
knows in his body his people's needs.
Your voice echoes still
through all the generations whom poverty crucifies.

> **Lord, by your cross and resurrection,
> you have set us free.**

It is accomplished.
(John 19:30)

Hope breaks
Through bleak despair.
No hatred, no persecution, no suffering, no death
can last forever,
Eternity is God's.

> **Lord, by your cross and resurrection,**
> **you have set us free.**

Jesus himself stood among them and said to them, 'Peace be with you!' But they were startled and frightened and supposed that they saw a spirit. And he said to them, 'Why are you troubled and why do questionings rise in your hearts? See my hands and my feet, that it is I myself . . . '
(Luke 24:36–39)

Signs of peace;
Your wounded hands and feet,
those witnesses to violence,
Now speak of healing and of hope
to the people you lead out of darkness
into the light of day.

> **Lord, by your cross and resurrection,**
> **you have set us free.**

Brentwood Diocesan Commission for Justice and Peace
England

Were You There When They Crucified the Lord?

Were you there when they crucified the Lord?
Yes, I was there.
Standing at the very edge of the crowd,
Pretending to be pausing on the way to somewhere else,
But in reality riveted
To what was happening to Jesus and those with him.

I saw Veronica's impetuous dash
To wipe the sweat from his face
And even as I condemned her action
For its display and lack of control and sheer futility –
I wished it could have been me.

I drew near then
I saw the way he looked
I saw his pain and humiliation
And saw – could it have been fear?
I saw his shattered body
Grotesquely hoisted without dignity
I heard him cry out
I heard the desperation in his voice
And for a moment I was moved to join
The crowd of mourners at his feet,
His mother, his friends and other nameless people.

But I suppressed my impulse,
I walked away.
Like the rich young man I grieved,
Unable to commit myself to him
That much courage, that much love,
I could not give.
Father, forgive me, for I knew what I was doing
I was there when they crucified the Lord.

Anthea Dove
England

203

Myrrh – A Reflection

Three Kings came
Cradled the Babe in bejewelled arms,
Gave of their gifts and left by a different path,
I wonder at their gifts as I
Cradle the Babe in homespun arms.

Gold is a useful gift.
The Babe likes the glitter and clink of it
And we are glad of the security it offers;
As we walk a different path to a new land.
I cradle the Babe in my lap
And wonder at God's mercy on it.

Frankincense – what to make of that then
Sweet smell and curled smoke rising.
A fitting sacrifice for God's Son in Jerusalem's Temple.
'A sword shall pierce my heart!'
I wonder at those two old dears and their words surprising.

Myrrh – myrrh causes my heart to tremble
As I cradle the Babe against my breast.
Myrrh betokens all the world's pain and all the world's loss
Anointing the dead – ah let me hold Him yet awhile –
Sweet, sweet child, grow not away too fast.
Abba, heavenly Father, let me know what is best.

Myrrh anoints all the world's pain and all the world's loss.
'Blessed are they who mourn for they shall be comforted!'
'Talithi cumi – give her something to eat.'
'If you want you can cure me.' 'Of course I want to be cured.'
'Do not cry. Young man, I say to you get up.'
As salve takes the sting from the pain
Abba's son and mine restore them to life again?

I wonder at this gift of myrrh
As I watch his body on the gibbet racked (wracked?).

My heart pierced by the pain he bears,
His head upon my breast and he, inert upon my lap.
Once more I embrace my son and wonder what we lacked
That Abba allowed it thus.

I wonder at this gift of myrrh
As I walk with the women to the tomb
How his body we need to anoint – the last comfort give.
And as I grasp the myrrh's portent; believe: in entering the
      pain
Break the barriers to find him living again.
Oh Abba, loving Father, Amen, Amen.

Anne Hine
England

The Repentant Thief

I think I had always expected it: the cross.
My father and two of my uncles had died that way after all,
And I was as bad as any of them, worse perhaps.
I could say I never had a chance,
My mother who was beautiful, warm and loving, but a bad lot
      too in her way I suppose,
            stoned to death by angry men.
I grew up with robbers. It was the way we lived,
Always hungry, always filthy,
Always angry with the rich, with life, with God.
But to be honest I knew all along
That there was something better,
That there was a better way to live.
It may have been the memory of my mother's tenderness,
An old man I had once seen praying fervently,
The unexpected sight of wild flowers, bright and lovely,
Or words overheard as I sneaked by the temple.
It may have been all of these things and others now forgotten,
But I cannot bring myself to pretend,

Pretend I was simply a victim of circumstance,
That I never had a choice,
That I couldn't help being a thief,
A man of violence,
A man without love.

Where tenderness, beauty and the name of God,
Glimpses of light in my muddled world,
Had touched me but failed to move me,
I was moved at last
When I saw him, Jesus, hanging near me on his cross.

His body was already half broken,
His face tortured, wet with blood and sweat and tears,
His eyes staring with pain, his mouth taut in agony.
The thief on the other side of him jeered,
And then, for the last time, in these last moments of my life,
I broke free.
I felt anger, as usual,
And, as never before, love.
I spoke. I don't know what I said,
Scolding the other fellow,
But looking at Jesus and feeling for him.
For the first time in my life I forgot myself.

He lifted his head and looked into my eyes,
In that moment I felt no pain from the cruel drag of the nails,
No fear, not even shame.
I felt empty, and then slowly filled
With light and warmth and love as he looked at me.
He could not smile, his voice was cracked and hoarse,
But his words and his meaning were unmistakable.
He said to me, Dismas, the most miserable of sinners,
'Today you will be with me in paradise.'
And then I knew joy.

Anthea Dove
England

What 'Good' is This?

Living Lord,
Was this the lifting high?
Humiliation seems complete:
forsaken by God;
deserted by friends;
mocked by many.
    And in our 'Holy Week'
    we call this 'Good'!
    What 'Good' is this?

Loving Lord,
you bore our shame:
in truth our names
inscribe the gallows wood.
    And in our 'Holy Week'
    we call this 'Good'
    What 'Good' this is!

Good for us:
your isolation for our community;
your capture for our freedom;
your life for our sin.
    And in this 'Holy Week'
    we call this 'Good'
    but not to gloss
    the pain endured
    as if your loss
    was somehow spared.

Stephen Brown
Scotland

Women of Jerusalem

We made ourselves walk alongside him, although it was almost more than we could bear to see him treated as a common criminal, staggering under that cross with blood running down his face.

This was Jesus, who knew us and loved us. Some of us women had been following the crowds for years, listening to his teaching, marvelling at his miraculous healings. Others of us had brought food for him and his disciples and washed and mended their clothes. And only five days ago we were so happy, cheering as he came into Jerusalem, riding on a donkey. I shouted till I was hoarse.

But now we were all silent, all weeping. Suddenly he lifted his face and looked straight at us. Even in his pain and fear and degradation, his eyes were full of compassion and he spoke directly to us saying,

'Daughters of Jerusalem, do not weep for me; weep rather for yourselves and your children.'

That was just like him.

Anthea Dove
England

Women at the Cross

Meanwhile near the cross of Jesus were his mother and his mother's sister, Mary the wife of Clopas and Mary Magdalene. (John 19:25)

> You are still God;
> upheld by those
> who remember you.
> The oppressed have always
> trusted you,
> and you have liberated them.
> When they cried

to you in trust,
you heard them
and did not reject them.

Janet Lees
England

O Sorrowful Women

O sorrowful women, a little distance from the cross!
How can we understand your profound sense of loss?
You look upon the loving Jesus, wounded beyond belief,
and know there is no way that you can give relief.
You see his loss of blood, the dreadful death he's dying
and you are huddled silent beyond the stage of crying.

O sorrowful Mary, you've fulfilled the mother's part
and now it seems a sword has pierced your heart.
From birth you cared for this your first-born son.
You taught him to walk, was glad to see him run.
You saw him grow in faith, in love and understanding
and while at home do everything at your commanding.

Most of the disciples have thought it best to hide
but, gently Mary, devoted John is at your side.
And from his cross Jesus says, 'Mother there is your son',
and to John, 'there is your Mother' — concern from one
now close to death, so very near to his last breath.
Thus John took Mary to his home the day of Jesus' death.

O sorrowful women, Jesus has died and still you stay,
for Joseph of Arimathaea has arrived to take away
the precious body now lowered from the cross.
Joseph too has his sad thoughts and sense of loss.
You follow him to the tomb, see the wrapped body placed there,
and then go home, perfumes and spices to prepare.

Rosemary S. Watts
England

On the Hillside She Stands Weeping

On the hillside she stands weeping
Standing, crying, watching keeping
Close to Jesus to the end.

Kyrie eleison, Lord have mercy on us
Kyrie eleison, Lord have mercy on us.

Oh such sadness, broken Mary
God's own mother, silently sees
Her own Son in agony.

Kyrie eleison, Lord have mercy on us
Kyrie elesion, Lord have mercy on us.

Help me sense what you are feeling
Make my spirit like yours burning
With the love of Christ my Lord.

Kyrie eleison, Lord have mercy on us
Kyrie elesion, Lord have mercy on us.

Paraphrase of Jacopone da Todi (d.1306)
and Edward Caswall (1814–1878)

Pat Livingstone
England

Modern Calvaries

You, whose flesh the cruel nails pierced
With fearful agonies,
O look with pitying eyes upon
Our modern Calvaries.

The weary centuries have fled
Since you were crucified.
Still Your love remains unheeded,
Your mercy is defied.

The pride of race and culture
That sets us all apart,
Are an offence against Your name
And must pierce You to the heart

Too many go unsheltered,
Too many go unfed,
All too many tears have flowed
For those too early dead.

Terrible along the city streets
Of near and distant lands,
Stained with the blood of innocence,
All too many crosses stand,

O You, whose earthly path was led
Through such pains to Easter Day,
In Your mercy grant that we
May walk the selfsame way.

O Love that willingly embraced
These fearful agonies,
With forgiveness look upon
Our modern Calvaries.

Doreen Gazey
England

211

A Good Friday Blessing

Bless you, Wise and Holy One,
for your enduring Word – the Word
that endures the cross of
    words heard
    but not understood
    palms bestowed
    for the wrong reason
    laurels withheld
    by home and family
    friends with us only
    until the cock crows
    peers who condemn
    our I-am-who-I-am-
    denounce our integrity
    as blasphemy.

Bless you, Wise and Holy One,
for your enduring Word from the cross –
    whoever is true to I-am-who-I-am
    who risks I-am for others
    rises from affliction
    rolls away despair
    endures beyond
    even death itself.

Norm S. D. Esdon
Canada

We Gaze on Crucifixion

*Following the Revd Dr John Taylor's reflection on
crucifixion at the Liverpool Methodist District Synod*

We gaze on crucifixion,
romanticise the fate:
the torn and tortured Jesus,
the brunt of human hate.

His heirs still rank among us
as children lie and bleed,
as parents cry in hunger,
the world still shouts its need.

The child that's torn by shrapnel,
the elderly denied,
the homeless and the hungry
are Jesus crucified.

7.6.7.6 metre

Andrew Pratt
England

Blessing the Thorn in the Flesh

Bless you, Wise and Holy One,
    for your Word made
    thorn in the flesh
for answering No when I prayed
    to have my thorn removed

Bless you
    for the thorn of alienation that
drives me deep into inner desert
    to face my need to please –

the desert where you re-create me
deeper than popularity
wider than the majority
truer than hypocrisy

Bless you
for the thorn of hardship that
helps me get the point –
that my thorn can serve
as another's therapy
that the best healer
is a wounded healer
that the hardship I cannot change
and that threatens to embitter me
can change me – for the better

Bless you, Wise and Holy One,
for this epiphany –
that praying away Good Friday
prays away Easter too

Bless you
for answering No when I pray
to have a thorn removed

Bless you, Wise and Holy One,
for your Word made
thorn in the flesh

Norm S. D. Esdon
Canada

Holy Saturday
The Waiting Time

'We walk by faith, not by sight.' (2 Corinthians 5:7)

Not Yet!

But not yet!
For this is a waiting time,
A strange and uncertain time:
A hard and a painful time,
    We wait in faith.
    We know the tale.
    We know the truth.
    But still we wait.
The wait is heavy.
Death deals our knockout blow.

Silence

And now our Lord and rock laid low,
the hope Christ prompted withered.
    We wait in faith.
    We know the tale.
    We know the truth.
    But still we wait.

The Christ cut down, the Cross still stands:
its rootless wood erect but dead.
A sacrifice for greater good,
the gallows grief is not the end.

We wait in faith.
We know the tale.
We know the truth.
But still we wait.

Stephen Brown
Scotland

Fourstep

Love king tied down
They mock, flog, nail,
Hang life upon tree,
Atop dung heap hill.

Seal body into tomb
Hard rock made door
Make sure this king
Lies dead, rock sure.

They wept over love,
Left with only fear,
Then life came back,
Tomb open, rock free.

From dead days rise,
Come into life anew,
Know that love wins,
God's word come true.

Colin Ferguson
England

What I Know

Once certain,
Now unsure,
The world I knew has gone.
What I know is that I do not know
Where I am going or
Who I am becoming.

What do I know?
I know that I breathe and sleep, laugh and cry;
I know the joy of love;
I know the pain of grief;
I know the emptiness of being vacant,
Waiting for the page to turn;
I know the grim determination to plough on despite
    the odds;
I know the fear of being lost.

. . . and yet . . .

I know that I am gently held
Called into new being by One
Who knows what I do not know –
Where I am going and
Who I am becoming.

Jane Cresswell
England

The Telegram

I went to the post office. A lady asked me to write out her telegram. She said, 'Write, "Gunman killed your nephew." '

I couldn't help looking at her face for a while in silence; but I could find nothing but numbness. It is still a picture in my head that does not go away.

217

The next morning, more bad news. Two little children and one old man were killed by a gunman in Hannah Town, Kingston, Jamaica, at 06.00. For 'political reasons'.

For as long as I live, I will never forget this uncivilised and irrational killing.

Byung-Joon Chung
Korea

God of My Faith

God of my faith, I offer you my doubt,
for life at times seems far too dark for me
and my belief becomes more insecure
when worldly cares produce uncertainty.

God of my hope, I offer you my fear,
when I am scared by my anxiety,
when all I hear is suffering and woe,
in all my shadows you will walk with me.

God of my joy, I offer you my grief,
when I sink down in sadness or despair,
when in depression I cannot be touched,
I pray in all my depths to find you there.

God of my love, I offer you my pain,
when I'm alone and feel nobody cares,
in aching age or in rejected youth,
you bear my cross and dry my human tears.

God of my life, I offer you my dreams,
light in the darkness when I hide from view,
light in my faith, my hope, my joy and love,
light in my life and all my life in you.

Colin Ferguson
England

The Morning After ... Saturday

Easter Saturday is all waiting. What do you do when God is in the grave? The morning after Good Friday is not Easter Sunday but this single, separate day when death seems to have won ...

A piece for three voices

Voice One: On the second day the crowds were sabbath-solemn and minding their own business.

Voice Two: On the second day Judas committed suicide because he could not forgive himself.

Voice One: On the second day Herod threw a party because no-one could blame him for anything.

Voice Two: On the second day Pilate smiled to himself because his wife was wrong – for once!

Voice One: On the second day the High Priest felt he could relax because he'd spent his money well.

Voice Two: On the second day the Pharisees and Sadducees congratulated each other that it was all over.

Voice One: On the second day the disciples locked the doors and planned their journeys home.

Voice Two: On the second day Peter knew he'd spoken out once too often and there was nothing he could do.

Voice One: On the second day Mary and the other women wept and wept and then prepared their spices.

Voice Two: On the second day the soldiers guarded the sealed grave and wondered why they bothered.

Voice Three: And on the third day Jesus said, 'What did I tell you ?'

Marjorie Dobson
England

He Waits in the Tomb

Whenever an innocent child is hurt
Whenever a plea is unheard
When we don't see the problems
for those who are deaf
or hear how the blind
haven't heard.
When arthritic hands
cannot grasp the book
when elderly bones
cannot kneel
and we wonder and stare
that the Lord didn't care
to make every one
just like us
He waits in the tomb.
For our hearts have grown hard
and we've chosen a way
that will lead us to angry defence
of a pitiless church
compassionless, cold,
violent, silent and tense.

Can't we see we are weak.
We're not clever or rich
just vulnerable folk
with a need
to reach out to the sick
and to side with the frail
and go down with the down and out.
For that's where our Lord is
despised, rejected, alone.
There he waits in the tomb
on the bus, in the queue
for asylum, a home,
or our heart.

Penny Bird
England

Easter Eve

Is this the hour the women waited
Feeling empty, flat, hopeless?
Only the one service left to perform and that to wait till
morning.

And I am come, at the end of this busy, empty, week
With its brief markers of Your pain, Your journey
Swallowed up in busyness or sleep.

Feeling that I should, at least, sit for an hour
Sense (distrusted) of You, close.

How can I both want, ache for You with this fierceness
Yet fight to keep You at arm's length, fearing Your intimacy?

Wendy White
England

Have You Left?

This Holy Saturday, this time of death in life is lived by many
    in our society for many reasons.
As Mary and the others left the place of crucifixion they
    entered a place
of grief, which is a place of dark numbness, no feeling risked,
    no future dared.

**Holy God, where have you roamed, why have you left your
    creation?**

The Hebrew people moaned in the wilderness.
What benefit is a grave in the wilderness over the graves of
    slavery?
By the waters of Babylon, they wept.
They couldn't sing to the Lord in a foreign land.

221

Holy God, where have you roamed, why have you left your creation?

There is no Gospel for today. There is no good news.
There is no purpose. Today there is no tomorrow.
And yesterday is too terrible for memories to comfort.
There is a void in me, in my friends, in the world.

Holy God, where have you roamed, why have you left your creation?

The desperate for food and drink cannot live before they die.
The elderly of our land dwell isolated in their homes.
The young hit out, to gain at least some human response.
And drugs numb the pain of rebel and polite suburb.

Holy God, where have you roamed, why have you left your creation?

The heart sinks to a deep fear when I hear of illness,
cancer, HIV and AIDS and cuts me off from friends and
    family.
My heart shrinks from those in the dark tunnel of mental
    torment.
There is this long waiting, this empty waiting for me and for
    them.

Holy God, where have you roamed, why have you left your creation?
The heart cries out. Can it dream of crying out to you ever again, Holy God?

John Ll Humphreys
Wales/Scotland

222

Part Four
Easter Day and Eastertide
A Time for Rejoicing

'Why do you look for the living among the dead?
He is not here; he has risen!' (Luke 24:5)

Easter Day
The Amazing, Joyful Experience

'I am with you always, to the very end of the age.' (Matthew 28:20)

God's New Life for the Whole World

May the God whose power breaks through the stone,
break into your life and free you from all that binds you;
May the Risen Christ whose love is stronger than death
speak your name and bring you new life and joy;
The Spirit who walks the road with you
give you wisdom to understand and courage to share
God's new life for the whole world.

Heather Pencavel
England

Roll Back the Stone

When we come running to your tomb today, Lord,
Dare we believe you are no longer there?
That now, set free from death's decaying shroud,
Your spirit soars exultant, spanning the universe,
and in the dawn, the yielding darkness heralds
a new creation on the brink of birth!

Shall we come boldly, hope-filled and expectant,
Singing our praises, shouting 'Alleluia'?
When we would cry aloud that you are risen –
Proclaim love's victory over pride and hatred –
from the constraints of order or tradition
roll back the stone!

Shall we come warily – hesitant and cautious –
longing to believe, yet shadowed by our doubt?
Lord, if we still seek you, lifeless, in the grave,
and fail to find you, vibrant, in the commonplace –
From the echoing chambers of our unbelief
roll back the stone!

Shall we stand weeping, overwhelmed by anguish –
not knowing where to turn – not recognising you?
If we are fearful, lonely or rejected
from the dank confines of our desperation
roll back the stone!

Come upon us quietly, Lord, and take us by surprise –
Speak our names and take our breath away!
Roll back the stone – release us from our mourning –
And through the amazing encounter of this Easter day
Impel us into joy.

Jill Jenkins
England

The Sharpened Chill, the Flower Strewn Tomb

The sharpened chill, the flower strewn tomb,
the early morning light,
the heavy stone had rolled away
the women, scared, took flight.

What happened in those latter days
to loosen fear tied tongues?
We only know grief turned to joy
and laughter filled their lungs.

Their utter grief was real enough,
the record rings as true,
and only time will tell if grief
can change for me and you.

That is our hope, but faith is hard
to grasp, or reconcile
with all that life has brought our way,
and joy is not our style.

Come to the centre of our pain
and sow the seeds of praise,
that, not denying anything,
your love might calm our days.

Any CM tune

Andrew Pratt
England

Running to Tell the Good News

We ran,
> how we ran,
>> How could we not?
>>> Knowing what we did,
>>>> Seeing what we had seen.
'Quick, Mary, Joanna, quick,
Pick up your skirts and run,
to tell, the others, the good news.'
Now!
> Now!
My heart will explode, surely,
> it is like falling in love,
>> only ten times greater,
>>> and running as well,
I feel as though
I will die –
No!
> No!
He is not dead,
> He is risen.

Wait! Wait! Wait till I see
Their faces
        light up with joy
'Mary, Joanna,   quick,   quick!'

Running, stumbling,
no longer in fear
but in joy!

Can you imagine?
My heart is beating
LOUD,   LOUD –
Can they hear it?
        Already – can they sense it?
                Already – do they know it?

Here, we are,
We have arrived.
I cannot talk, breathless, joy,   too great,
I manage,   hardly,   to utter the words:
'He is risen' and again, 'HE IS RISEN!'

And as I stop
to catch my breath,
I see,
the men –
their faces
        dull and dismayed,
and their eyes
do not
        light up
but look only
as if to say:
'What are we
        to do
                with these
                hysterical
                        women?'

Susy Brouard
England

228

Mary in the Garden

I met Him in the darkness
Of the early morn.
The quiet expectant darkness
That comes before the dawn.
But night to me was endless.
The sun would never rise
And I did not recognise Him
When He stood before my eyes.

I asked, 'Who are you, my master?'
He said, simply, 'I am life.'
I am the Life that has died.
I am the Love that was slain.
The light that was crucified.
I died and I rose again
For the Light can never be conquered.
My Love can never die
And I shall always be with you
To the end of time.

Doreen Gazey
England

Easter Gardens

Bright Spring sunshine,
Streams across the lawns,
Sunlight enhances the colours,
Daffodils reaching upwards toward heaven,
Golden trumpets proclaim the news,
Christ is risen
For this is my Easter garden.

Modern pilgrims from across the world,
Visit modern tempestuous Jerusalem,
Churches and shrines proliferate,

Built over holy sites
The tomb remains on the hillside,
Standing in its own grounds,
It is the enduring Easter garden.

What flowers bloomed this morning?
As furtive figures
Approached the tomb in trepidation.
Exotic, perfumed blooms,
Adorning the borders,
Tribute to those who tended them,
The original Easter garden.

Mary Magdalene was distraught,
The tomb was empty,
Not able to embalm her lord,
yet through tear-obstructed vision
she glimpsed the figure of a man,
mistakenly addressed him as a gardener,
who tended the Easter garden.

Suddenly everything changed forever,
One spoken word, Mary.
Instant response, Master.
The Lord is risen,
Speaking to Magdalene.
Whose heart is overflowing
In the joyful Easter garden.

Northern Spring symbol of new life,
Adding colour to our celebration,
Proclaiming Christ's great victory,
The winter of the soul is past,
That vibrant life returns to the living world,
Vibrant hope exploding to blossom
in the everlasting Easter garden.

Y. Mochyn Daear
England

230

I Have Seen the Lord

John 20:1–23; 11–18

Blessed Jesus, known to Mary Magdalene as human friend and as Risen Lord, give me a portion of the love which brought her to your feet on Resurrection morning. Cast out the evil things that lurk in my life, give me the constancy that follows to the end and grant me at last the full glory of your presence which I now know by faith.

Raymond Chapman
England

Mary Magdalene's Story

I wake very early. With waking, comes instant awful memory. The realisation that it isn't all a bad dream. It's true. He's dead. Dead. The only man who had been able to give me back my self-esteem, who, from our very first meeting looked at me with respect. The first man to show me compassion and understanding, and love. He has taught me a completely new meaning to the word love. Now he's gone.

Killed by Roman soldiers, but Pilate was right to wash his hands. His blood is not on their hands, but on those of the so-called leaders of the Jewish faith, the self-righteous Pharisees. They were so busy looking down their long noses at sinners like me, they failed to recognise that the Messiah, the one they had been preaching about and waiting for, was here – living and working among us. They simply saw him as a threat to their power – so they had him crucified. That long agonising death. I shall never forget it. As long as I live whenever I close my eyes, I will see that picture of him, hanging on the cross and hear him saying those incredible words:

'Father, forgive them, they do not know what they are doing.'

I get up and carefully carrying a jar of spikenard, I go outside. The dawn will soon break; there are red streaks in the sky bringing the promise of a beautiful day. But, no day will ever be beautiful again – without him.

Joanna, Salome and Mary are coming down the road carrying their jars of oils and spices. We arranged to meet this morning and go to the tomb, as there is just one thing left that we can do for him. We do not speak. Words would be irrelevant. Just a quick hug, then we go on our way. It's not far and soon we arrive at the garden. Joanna suddenly remembers the heavy stone that the soldiers had put over the entrance and they would be guarding the tomb. We realise that we have not really thought this thing through, maybe we can persuade the soldiers to move the stone for us. Some of them were quite sympathetic to Jesus at the crucifixion. The sun is just coming up over the hill as we approach the tomb. We stop and stare, unable to believe what our eyes are seeing. The stone, the big, heavy stone has been rolled away and there is no sign of any soldiers. He's gone! Now even his body is gone and I am denied this one last thing that I was going to do for him. The others run back to tell Peter and the rest of them what has happened, but I can only stand there with the tears running down my face. I stoop down and look inside. The grave clothes are neatly folded and there seems to be some kind of a bright light shining. I hear a voice behind me:

'Why are you crying? Who are you looking for?'

'Are you the gardener? Have you taken him away? Please tell me where he is. I must do this one last thing for him,' I reply.

Then I hear a voice that I thought I would never hear again say:

'Mary.'

I turn round.

'Rabboni,' I answer, hardly daring yet to believe what I am hearing. I reach out my hands to him, but he says:

'Do not touch me yet. First, I have to go back to my Father. Go and tell Peter and the other disciples that you have seen me.'

I wipe my tears away. He is gone.

But, of all the people in the world, at this moment, I am the only one who knows that Jesus is alive. I have seen him. He came first to me. Now I must do as he says, go, and tell the others.

Heather Johnston
Scotland

Mary Magdalene's story could be presented dramatically, with children miming the story as it is read, as part of this all age worship.

At an activity session prior to Easter Sunday, children can make a life-size Easter garden and tomb, using a tent frame, green drapes, branches, cardboard stone etc.

Processional Hymn: 'Lord of the Dance'

Some children carry a cross,
some carry flowers for Easter Garden
some carry plates of Easter biscuits
some wave streamers
Place cross at front
Put biscuits on table
Put flowers in garden and roll away the 'stone'
Light Easter Candle.

Easter Responses

Leader: *(Lights candle)* **The Lord is risen.**

All: **He is risen indeed**.

Drama: 'Mary Magdalene's Story'

Song: 'The Stone was Rolled Away'

Prayers

Song: 'He is Lord'

Hymn: 'This joyful Easter Time', *as children leave for:*

Easter Egg Hunt:

Children are told that hidden around the church hall(s) and outside (if weather and situation are appropriate) are some cream eggs. Their task is to find them all while the adults listen to the next part of the service. Leaders can go with them to help and put them into baskets and when they hear the next hymn playing, go back in and children can distribute the eggs to all the congregation. (Leaders make sure that there are sufficient eggs for all adults and enough left over for the children! So have a supplementary supply ready, otherwise you might need the loaves and fishes miracle!)

Easter Reflection/Address

Hymn: 'Christ the Lord is Risen Today'

Blessing

Refreshments: Coffee/tea/squash/biscuits – including Easter ones if made.

Heather Johnston
Scotland

It is the Lord

John 21:1–7

Bringing life from death
Bringing abundance from nothing
Bringing confidence from doubt

It is the Lord.

234

Loving the poor, the weak, the failed,
Loving the foreigner, the stranger, the unwanted,
Loving the people, both friends and opponents

It is the Lord.

Calling us to take the risk that we will change nothing
Calling us to step out in deep waters
Calling us to faith

It is the Lord.

Changing the ordinary to the extraordinary
Changing an obstacle into an opportunity
Changing our weakness into great strength

It is the Lord.

Risen Lord,
You love us,
You call us,
You change us.
Let us recognise your coming
However gently or dramatically you approach us.
Let us recognise your coming
Whoever you use to make yourself known to us.
Let us recognise your coming
Whatever time or situation you use to approach us.
Let us recognise your compassionate emergence
Into the dark places of our lives,
Your generous summons which you constantly utter,
Your transforming touch upon the bleak places of
our world.
Lord of life, of hope, of resurrection,
We make our prayer in your name, Jesus,
Amen

Brentwood Diocesan Commission for Justice and Peace
England

235

Resucito

Resucito!

He
    is
       Risen!

And He makes His home
in me.

I do not have to invite Him,
implore Him,
or beg Him enter in.

He is
already there.
Within my vulnerable, wounded self
the Christ has made His home;
fulfilling divine destiny
through my inadequate
humility.

Infinitesimally closer is He
than I
could ever imagine.

Resucito. He is risen.

And He is

    Alive.

I am alive:
No longer I, but Christ in me.

Pat Marsh
England

In Christ's Rising from the Dead

In the sprouting of the seed,
In the fruiting of the flower
    We celebrate new life
    And live the Easter faith.

In the wonder of a birth,
In the laughter of a child,
    We celebrate new life
    And live the Easter faith.

In the coming of our worth,
In the caring for ourselves,
    We celebrate new life
    And live the Easter faith.

In the linking with the past,
In the presence of the dead,
    We celebrate new life
    And live the Easter faith.

In Christ's rising from the dead,
In God's bursting from the tomb
    We celebrate new life
    And live the Easter faith.

W. L. Wallace
Aotearoa New Zealand

Do Not Be Afraid

In your way, transforming God,
creation is forever moving:
    A wilderness becomes a sea;
    angry clouds become pillars of smoke;
    the dust of pursuit is settled;
    and an ocean of despair becomes a path to explore.

In your way, disturbing God,
everything is turning:
    The deadness of morning becomes an angel light;
    the pitch of a tomb becomes a tunnel;
    the death of fear becomes the life of a dance;
    and all the ghosts that pursue us are washed away.

Help us walk your way,
    Today, as every day:
    self-confidence melts to terror;
    fear turns to joy;
    and a voice speaks through the confusion;
    'Do not be afraid!'

Help us hear the voice,
    Like the Israelites,
    like the women,
    we are called to rise up,
    and walk forward.
    Follow the way.
    Follow the light.
    Follow the love.

Rise up
For he is risen.

Duncan Tuck
England

Hope

We need hope for the future
in our nostalgia
for half-forgotten summer days
long past.

We need hope of pardon
in our regrets
which drift through our minds
like autumn clouds of dying leaves.

We need hope of comfort
in our fears and anxieties
fed by the long hours of darkness
in winter.

Hope of the World,
born in dark midwinter,
give us hope
at your coming
so that we may be newly created
With you on Easter Day.

Mary Brogan
England

Follow in Humility

Bartholomew was a witness of the Resurrection

Blessed Lord, teach me to serve without desiring any reward
except to do your will. As Bartholomew was obedient and was
made a witness of the Resurrection, so let me follow in humility
until I come to share in that eternal life.

Raymond Chapman
England

Alleluias Echoed

Alleluias echoed,
our songs of praise ran high,
but that was in another time,
now darkness clouds the sky.

The tears that we will cry,
the shroud of grief we wear,
are evidence of sundered love,
of all we have to bear.

As Mary wept for Christ,
while grief was sharp and raw,
so now we feel akin with her
through all we felt, and saw.

God sow a seed of hope,
and give us, through your grace,
the merest essence of your love
to resurrect our faith.

Any SM tune

Andrew Pratt
England

He Has Won the Peace

He has won the peace by his death on the cross, a peace offered
to us, a peace which is costly, risky and demands vulnerability
but it brings a joy and delight which the world's peace secured
by the threat to annihilate our enemies can never bring. May
Easter be in our minds and hearts and in the minds and hearts
of all peoples.

Gerard W. Hughes
England

Easter Morning

Walking in the garden
among blood-red tulips
heads down-drooping,
beside triumphant golden trumpets
shading purple pansies at their feet,
faces upturned in adoration
a sparrow chirrups
blue-tits chatter
searching, gathering, building.

Spring rain falls gently
causing tadpoles to twirl
and fish to leap
from dark depths into light.

A train speeds by
uniting friends and relations,
a mother calls her children –
they run in, hiding sticky fingers
but their chocolate smiles give them away.

Walking in the garden
I pick a pungent sprig of rosemary
for the Easter lamb.

Heather Johnston
Scotland

Easter Sunday

Rows of chocolate coated eggs
line the supermarket shelves
What have they to do with Easter?
you may ask yourselves.

Look out of the window
What do you see? Birds
their beaks bursting with moss and straw
building busily.

What's it like inside a bird's egg?
Is it scary in the gloom?
What was it like for Jesus
inside that rocky tomb?

But the egg will soon crack open
a new life is beginning
Like Jesus rising from the tomb
On that first Easter morning.

Heather Johnston
Scotland

We Are an Easter People

We are an Easter people,
Ours is an Easter faith,
    The yeast is rising in our hearts
    Our wine has vintage taste –
Christ is risen,
Christ is risen,
Risen in our lives.

We are an Easter people,
Ours is an Easter faith,

Our tears are freed to flow and heal
Our shattered hopes and hearts –
Christ is risen,
Christ is risen,
Risen in our lives.

We are an Easter people,
Ours is an Easter faith,
Our fears have died, we rise to dream,
To love, to dance, to live –
Christ is risen,
Christ is risen,
Risen in our lives.

W. L. Wallace
Aotearoa New Zealand

Being Dead Already

Being dead already
I had no need of the fear
That had constricted me
Like a winding shroud.

I wondered at first
Why I felt so free
Then I realise I had forgotten it
And left it behind in the grave.

'Couldn't I go back and tell them
They won't need their fear either?'
I suggested.
'That's just what I *did*,'
he said.

Cecily Taylor
England

The First Easter
I Was There (1)

Suitable for children to present for an assembly or all age worship

Cast:	*Peter, Centurion, Mary – Jesus' mother, John, Mary Magdalene and Chorus (any number of people – a percussion accompaniment could be used)*
Chorus	Were you there, were you there? Who are you, who are you? What did you see, what did you hear? What did you say, what did you do?
Peter	I'm Peter, one of Jesus' best friends. I was there that first Easter, which started so horribly and ended so wonderfully. One thing that I remember is that after Jesus was arrested I was very frightened and when people asked me if I was one of Jesus' friends, I lied three times and said that I didn't know him and had never met him. Even worse, was the fact that Jesus had told me I would do this and I said 'No way, Lord, I'd even die for you.' I am very ashamed about this but Jesus forgave me and asked me to start his church, which I did.
Chorus	Were you there, were you there? Who are you, who are you? What did you see, what did you hear? What did you say, what did you do?
Centurion	I'm a Roman Centurion, I was there on duty when Jesus was crucified. I've been at many crucifixions but none has ever touched me the way this one did. Jesus was so different. He even asked his God to forgive us for what we had done to him and then I knew that he was really the Son of God and I wanted to believe in him too.

244

Chorus	Were you there, were you there?
	Who are you, who are you?
	What did you see, what did you hear?
	What did you say, what did you do?

Mary I'm Mary, Jesus' mother, so of course I was there. It was terrible for me to see him suffering on that cross. I would willingly have suffered the pain for him if I could, because that's how we mothers feel about our sons and daughters. From the moment they are born, we just want them to be happy and healthy. I knew that Jesus was special because he was God's son and I had a feeling that he would have to go through great pain before he returned to God.

Chorus	Were you there, were you there?
	Who are you, who are you?
	What did you see, what did you hear?
	What did you say, what did you do?

John I'm John and I was one of Jesus' best friends too. I was there with Mary when Jesus was on the cross and Jesus told me to look after his Mum and of course, I said I would. That was just like Jesus, always thinking of others, even when he was dying. I was also there with Peter on the first Easter Sunday. We went to the tomb in the garden where Jesus' body was put and we found it empty and we remembered that Jesus had said he would come back from the dead on the third day, so we rushed off to tell the others.

Chorus	Were you there, were you there?
	Who are you, who are you?
	What did you see, what did you hear?
	What did you say, what did you do?

Mary Magdalene	I'm Mary Magdalene, I was one of a group of women who followed Jesus. He was the most wonderful person you could ever meet; he made me feel I was someone special at a time when I was not feeling good about myself. After he died on the cross, I felt as though my life had finished too. I went to the garden and Jesus himself appeared to me. So, I was the first person to see him alive and to tell all his friends that he was alive.
Chorus and Cast	We were there, we were there, We saw Jesus crucified We were there, we were there, When Jesus came alive So we can be joyful, we can all say Happy Easter – Jesus is alive today.

Heather Johnston
Scotland

I Was There (2)
The Women Who Were There

Singers	Were you there when they crucified my Lord? Were you there when they crucified my Lord? Oh, sometimes it causes me to tremble, tremble, tremble, tremble; Were you there when they crucified my Lord?
St Veronica	Yes. I am Veronica. I was there. Legend says that I met Jesus on the way to his crucifixion. I looked at his poor bleeding body, bent double under the weight of the cross. I looked on his pain-filled face, running with sweat and streaked with blood and dirt. I ran up to him, dodging out of the way of the soldiers. I took off

the linen cloth covering my head and wiped his face. He looked at me smiled, said 'thank you' and staggered on. When I looked at the cloth, a picture of Jesus' face was imprinted on it. A little blue flower, the speedwell, is also called Veronica, because it is as though the blue of the sky is mirrored on its petals, just like Jesus' face was mirrored on my piece of cloth.

Singers Were you there when they nailed him to the tree? . . .

Salome Yes. I am Salome. I was there. I felt bad enough watching them nail my nephew, Jesus, to the cross, knowing how terribly he was going to suffer, so how much worse must it have been for his mother, Mary, my sister. I tried to comfort and support her as best as I could. I couldn't help thinking of that time when I asked Jesus for special places in heaven for my sons, James and John, and he made me see, in such a gentle, loving way that I was wrong to be ambitious for them. He said that we must learn to serve others if we want to be great. Then he said that he himself came to serve and give his life for others. I am so glad that my son, John, was there and Jesus told him to take care of Mary, his mother, as if he were her son. I was proud to share him with her.

Singers Were you there when they pierced him in the side? . . .

Mary Magdalene Yes. I am Mary Magdalene. I was there. My heart was breaking. How could they do this to the man who, in his short life had done so much for so many people? His whole life was one of love. His love was able to cast out the demons that had haunted my life, he gave me back my

	self-esteem and I became one of a small band of women who travelled with him. He was different from other men; he had a respect and regard for women that made us feel equal, not second-class citizens.
Singers	Were you there when the sun refused to shine? . . .
Mary	Yes. I am Mary, the mother of Jesus. I was there. My heart was as bleak and heavy as the sky. I think I always knew, even on the strange night of his birth, in that stable in Bethlehem that he was born to suffer for us all. I knew that he didn't deserve to be hanging on that cross, but I knew that somehow it had to be. It was all a part of God's plan to show his love for all the world and I had to be there with him to show him that a mother's love is always there for her son, and even in his suffering, he thought about me and asked John to take care of me.
Singers	Were you there when they laid him in the tomb? . . .
All Women	Yes. We were there. We followed them as they took his body to the tomb in the garden.
Singers	Were you there when God raised him from the dead? . . .
Mary Magdalene	Yes. I was there first. I actually saw him. He spoke to me.
All Women	Hallelujah! Christ is risen. Our Lord is alive today.

Heather Johnston
Scotland

Risen Christ

Risen Christ
As you stay with us
Open our eyes to see the needs in your world,
Open our ears to hear the cries
of the poor
of the suffering
the marginalised
give us the courage and the tenacity to take our spoken
    prayers into serious action.
Move us from our security
To take risks just like Jesus
And as you want us to do now
To walk with humankind
Knowing that you, Spirit of God, will support us
As we meet you please
Re-assure
Re-new
And re-commit us to a life of service
With no strings attached
Where we will stand for justice and peace
Risen Christ, on this Easter Day may things change
    because of us.
Amen

Geoffrey Duncan
England

A Tree in Galilee

A tree once grew in Galilee
Where birds sang unafraid,
And blossoms bloomed along each bough –
The children loved its shade.

The tree grew strong in Galilee,
But when the summer came
Some people tried to break it down
With dark and deadly aim.

The blossoms fell, the birds had flown,
Except for one white dove;
They cut the branches like a cross
To hang the Prince of Love.

Oh, there they hanged the Prince of Love
And took him down for dead,
But when the winter's hold was scarce three days,
Then spring burst out instead.

New life burst out for joy again,
The birds sang loud and free
While petals fell like blessings from
That tree in Galilee.

And where they fall is healing love,
Who climb it find new birth,
Its roots can touch the hearts of all,
Its branches span the earth.

Cecily Taylor
England

The Rose

How silently
how silently the rose
from nothingness in bud appears
and piano
pianissimo
it bursts blood-petalled
silently manwards
and thirsts for hallowed recognition . . .
then blown
returns to dust
assured of resurrection.
How silently
how silently the rose . . .

Harry Wiggett
South Africa

The Power of Your New Life

Risen Lord,
    be with me in the power of your new life,
Open me that I may grow in the Spirit
    in love and understanding,
    in knowledge and self-giving.
Let me receive your strength
    that I may accept your trials
    which I must endure with you.
Help me to treasure the revelations you bring
    of the presence and power
    of God.
Give me the refreshment
    of a new beginning
    in his joy and glory.

Paul Iles
England

251

Love of Jesus, Fill Me

Love of Jesus, fill me,
Joy of Jesus, surprise me,
Peace of Jesus, flood me,
Light of Jesus, transform me,
Touch of Jesus, warm me,
Strength of Jesus, encourage me,
        O Saviour, in your agony, forgive me,
in your wounds hide me,
and in your risen life take me with you,
for love of you and of your world.
Amen

Angela Ashwin
England

Mary's Courage

*It was Mary Magdalene who went to the tomb, she went by herself.
It was Mary Magdalene who went to fetch Peter and the other
disciple.
But they left. They had seen the tomb. They waited for nothing else.
It was Mary Magdalene who stayed. She wept. She fought with her
grief. She struggled with angels. She interrogated the gardener. She
wanted to know.*

*Jesus said her name. 'Mary'. She lived again as her name was
spoken. Mary Magdalene turned to Jesus. 'Rabbouni!' She went to
hug him. Jesus, her friend, her teacher, her companion, her Lord –
alive. Naturally, after the nightmare of separation, injustice and
death, she went to hug him, to hold him so as never to be separated
again.*

*Jesus said: 'Do not hold on to me, because I have not yet ascended to
the Father.'
How hard those words sounded to Mary. After everything, she never
wanted to lose him.*

Jesus turns her from the past to the future. 'Go and tell them . . .'
Mary, the marginalised woman, went to announce Easter.
Courageously she looked to the future. He is risen!

Jesus is risen! Alleluia!
The gloom is lifted, but we are told not to hold on to him!
Holy God, help us to have Mary's nerve,
wrestling with angels, questioning and announcing Easter.
Give us the courage to speak, show and share Easter
with each other, with all the brokenness of the world,
not with a trite smile but with a deep passion
for the dignity of the human community, of each individual.
Give us such courage, that like the disciples we may hear
from the Marys of our world that tomorrow is for you to
make.
May we not hold on to what comforts us,
but turn from what was;
towards what with you is still to be.

John Ll Humphreys
Wales/Scotland

Eastertide
After the Time of Doubt ...
the Time of Knowing

'The Lord became flesh and dwelt among us.
We have seen his glory.' (John 1:14)

Encounter with Us Now Enlivening God

Behind locked doors
Those who have met the risen Christ
Seek the security of bolts and bars.

And Thomas, unconvinced by their assertions,
demands to touch the nail-torn hands
and trace the spear's intrusion.
Till, faced with living proof,
Crying in wonder, 'My Lord and my God'
He hears the blessing given
to all who, from that time,
must come to faith unsighted.

Out in the public places, teaching in the Temple,
Countering jesters and judges, scholars and stone-throwers,
Confronting authority with courage and assurance –
The spirit-filled apostles, with hearts on fire,
and tongues let loose, proclaim God's saving grace,
and in Christ's name bring healing and renewal.

Encounter with us now, enlivening God,
Spring us from the safety-net of our sanctuaries;

Expose us to the challenge of your gospel;
Coax us to throw our caution to the winds.
May we, who name ourselves Christ's followers today,
Embody the command to be his witnesses,
The gathered company scattered to make known your truth,
to teach and tend, revive and reconcile.
Confirm our faith and send us out rejoicing
because we have put our trust
in your liberating power.

Jill Jenkins
England

Along the Way

Come with us, Lord,
along the Emmaus Road of everyday.

Increase our understanding
as we walk the way with you.

Fill our hearts with love
that we may serve others better;
and when evening comes
stay with us
and be known to us
in deepening communion with you.
Amen

Cecily Taylor
England

Believing

'Unless I see and touch'
For seeing is believing.
That was Thomas' reaction.

255

How often has it been ours?
In agreement with him,
Whose name is synonymous with doubt.

Risen Lord you still appear,
Not in the locked room,
Of my inner being.
Gazing at me from the printed page,
Framed in a child's face,
Yet hope still rises from despair.

It is your presence Lord,
In this broken world,
That prevents total self-destruction,
Masochistic mutilation is rife!
Yet not as deep as your wounds,
Endured to bring salvation.

Y. Mochyn Daear
England

My Lord and My God

John 20:24–29

Jesus Christ, my Lord and my God, forgive my hesitation, my
doubt, my uncertainty. May I learn from the experience of
blessed Thomas that the Good News is true in the times of
desolation as in the times of devotion. As I have known you to
be my Saviour, keep me firm in that knowledge and let me
make your glory known to others who are seeking the way.

Raymond Chapman
England

The Stranger on the Shore

The stranger on the shore that morning
waited for the returning fishermen
who had trawled all night and caught nothing.

Fishing meant hard, exhausting effort
struggling with straining nets
hauling in the heavy, heaving catch
from the treacherous, skin-drenching sea.

Beaching the boats, tired and dejected,
They heard his confident prediction –
'Cast out your nets again, the other side . . . '
And soon the shoals leapt, shining, in the mesh
like living shards of silver.

Dragging the catch ashore,
They found the stranger waiting –
Stranger no longer, but their familiar friend
Breaking the bread . . . inviting them to share . . .
The common meal made holy in his hands.

And then the questions, searching Peter's soul –
'Turn now, and face me – do you love me still?
Then be the guide and guard of all my sheep,
Denial is done; take courage.
Follow me.'

The stranger on the Damascus road
Challenging Saul to face his bigotry
Laid claim upon his life – 'Acknowledge who I am.
Your hate no longer blinds you.
Follow me'.

Stranger and friend, you take us unawares,
Flawed as we are, unwilling, ill-prepared
To be the people we profess to be.
Forgive and bless us; open hands and hearts
To give with grace and share without reserve.

Absolve the past; affirm your promise to us –
'I chose you and I love you –
Follow me'.

Jill Jenkins
England

Voyage of Discovery

At sunset the boat slipped out,
Criss-crossing the lake,
Seeking the shoals.
Peter knew these waters
Like the back of his hand.
That is why he had come,
Seeking solace in the familiar
Yet no sooner had he spoken
'I am going fishing'
He was joined by others,
Seven in all, with one resolve,
Trying to make sense of things
Following familiar patterns.

Will it help them forget?
Gain clearer insights?

Hours pass without success.
Suddenly it's day-break
Revealing a figure in the mist
Words are exchanged, action follows.
Net cast once again, on the other side.
Hauled ashore, full to breaking point.
Failure turned into success
Realisation dawns.
At the water's edge stands the Risen Christ!
Weary workers find bread and a fire.
Time to share food and fellowship with the Lord.
Jesus is here in Galilee

As he said he would be.
In the work-a-day world.
Breakfasting with the night shift . . .
Christ is risen
engaging with all humanity.

Y. Mochyn Daear
England

Mary's Remembering

Sometimes as I wander by the sea, near Magdala, I remember.
There is a lot to remember – the fishing boats, the call – my call
to follow.
And I did.
As the sea washed over my tired feet I remember that I
poured my soothing precious oil on his feet; my own offering,
the best I had.
And he was glad but Judas was angry, 'a waste' he said, he
was so keen on money for this and that and in the end he
betrayed his own friend.
Jesus was kind . . . glad. He said what I had done would be
remembered.
Perhaps it will, perhaps it won't.
But what Jesus did will be remembered. He died on a cross
and I was there. No oil on his poor feet than, no men to be
angry – just we women and John of course, staying to the end.
We watched him die,
we saw him laid to rest.
We were witnesses to his coming again.
But now I wander by the shore and think of all our feet have
done.
The walking beside, the refreshing, the anointing, the pain
and the following. We have been forgotten for a while but our
feet and our hearts march on.

Elizabeth Bradley
England

259

Tomb Day

It's a tomb day alright,
miserable and raining,
dreary and dull.
Bored, I go downstairs
to do my ironing
and think of Mary,
going back to
John's house
and getting on
with life.
On the outside,
nothing's changed,
but on the inside,
everything.
I think of her,
cooking, cleaning,
washing,
hanging out
the clothes
to dry
and
all the time
thinking,
wondering,
questioning,
remembering,
her son,
that once
was hers,
and

is

no
more.

Susy Brouard
England

Who Would Have Believed It . . .

This was performed in a service at a conference which was looking at world development issues. We looked at having belief in difficult circumstances. Part 1 was performed outside the church. It was dusk. The two actors hid behind a hedge so that the congregation only heard their voices.

Part 2 was played out towards the end of the service in the church. Actors memorised their lines.

Acting Parts:

| Part 1: | Disciple |
| | Thomas |

Part 2:	Disciple
	Thomas
	James
	Peter
	John
	A group of disciples

Part 1

Disciple	I'm so sorry that you weren't with us the other night.
Thomas	I know, I know – but it was difficult.
Disciple	I didn't really mean that. I meant . . .
Thomas	Look, I did my best, but it was getting dark.
Disciple	I know, I know.
Thomas	Was everyone there?
Disciple	Oh yes.
Thomas	Well, that's good . . . Did anyone miss me ?
Disciple	Thomas – Jesus was there.
Thomas	Don't talk about Him that way. It hurts too much.

Disciple	*(Quietly)* Look I'm sorry Thomas, I'm not trying to hurt you. He really was there. We were all there and he came. He was there.
Thomas	Don't. Please don't. I can hardly bare to think about him. I don't want it. *(Angry and hurt)* I don't want this death. *(Shouts)*
Disciple	I know, I didn't believe Mary either, but now I do, because I've spoken to Him.
Thomas	You're really serious, aren't you? *(Incredulous)*
Disciple	He was there, Thomas. The door was locked. They might have found us. You never know.
Thomas	Well, you're talking nonsense then, aren't you?
Disciple	No, no. He just came. I don't know how or where from. He was just suddenly there, telling us that we're to go just as He did.
Thomas	I can't believe this!
Disciple	He greeted us as ever with 'Peace be with you.' And he breathed on us.
Thomas	Huh! This is mad. Hysterical women, and deluded men. I won't believe it.
Disciple	Of course you don't have to, but you're wrong.
Thomas	I won't believe it unless I see the nail marks in his hands and put my finger where the nails were and put my hand into his side, I will not believe it. *(Angry)*

Part 2

Most of the disciples are already in the room. Greet others (ad lib as they arrive.

Thomas	It'll be good to see the others tonight.
Disciple	Yes, yes it's always good to be together. *(Knock on the door)*
James	*(Opens the door)* Oh good, good to see you.
Thomas	Is everyone coming ?

262

James	Yes, they're all here. Let's lock up now. *(Bolts the door)*
	(Disciple and Thomas greet the other disciples, embrace, shake hands, wave across the room)
Thomas	Oh, good to see you.
John	You too.
Disciple	Hi! *(Embraces another brother)*
	(As this goes on Jesus quietly enters)
Peter	Jesus!
Jesus	Peace be with you!
	. . . Thomas.
Thomas	Lord.
Jesus	Thomas. Here, look at my hands, put your finger here. Reach out your hand and put it into my side. Stop doubting and believe.
Thomas	My Lord and my God.
Jesus	Because you have seen me, you have believed. Blessed are those who have not seen and yet have believed.

Pat Livingstone

We Would Be an Easter People

'Easter people' is the appellation used by St Augustine for those who followed Jesus.

We would be an Easter people
living resurrection now,
make two thousand years of promise
real as Jesus shows us how.

Meeting Mary Jesus loved her,
calling to her by her name.
Those who need the love of Jesus
we will welcome just the same.

263

'Peace be with you' was Christ's greeting
to the ones who'd let him die.
May our greeting be as gracious
to the ones who'd spurn our cry.

Doubting Thomas was confounded:
Jesus loved him in his doubt.
Help us welcome saint and sceptic
as we work your purpose out.

Let us live the resurrection
in each time, in every place.
Let us live as Easter people,
true to Jesus' boundless grace.

8.7.8.7 metre

Andrew Pratt
England

Jesus Appears to His Mother After His Death

After three days of noise.
The silence came like an onslaught;
It came hushed and whispered
Like the first time
When the angel had appeared
Only this time it was something too great to comprehend.

I did not have to look then,
Either in the room or the empty tomb.
I knew,
And sitting patiently in John's house
I felt a presence, like that of a silent bird
Alighting on the window-sill.

It would have been too much therefore,
to turn around and see you.
Already my joy was so great
That it felt as though
The double-edged sword
Was being pierced through
My heart again.

It was enough, then
To feel your loving presence
Surround me like a mantel
And your breathing become
Like that of a sleeping child
Oh, peace!

Susy Brouard
England

The Cock Crowed Twice

You are Peter – 'Rocky Stone'
On you I'll build my church
There'll be men of sand
Determined to stand
Dependable, solid and firm

There'll be men so firm
They'll distort my love
And mangle it with fear

There'll be men of fear
Whose authority stands
By terror and by pain

Merciless, pitiless
In empathy sightless
Defending rocks and stone

I will take away your heart of stone
And give you a heart of flesh
Experience will teach you
Rape, terror and grief
Rejected, abused and dumb

Awareness so keen
That the lance of love
Will pierce at each new wrong

Truth, lighting each horror
Will rock the church
And bring the terror down

Now, feed my lambs
With your heart of flesh
And shelter them, dear Stone.

Penny Bird
England

A Blessing in the Resurrection Season

God has led us from slavery
to the freedom of the blessed of God
God had led us through the water of death
to the gospel shore of life
God is leading us from the horror of war
to the peace of the bosom of Christ.

May the risen Christ give us the joy of eternal life.
Amen

Let us bless the Lord! Alleluia! Alleluia!
Thanks be to God! Alleluia! Alleluia!

Vaughan Jones
England

God of Love

God of love enfold us,
God of comfort heal us.
God of joy uplift us,
God of hope renew us,
God of peace refill us
Time and time again.

Cecily Taylor
England

Thomas

Thank you, Lord, for Thomas –
  not there,
  not sure,
  left out when the others saw the risen Lord.

Risen Lord, be with us, we pray, when we fail to see you;

when we want to believe
    but can only see legend and myth,
    and are tempted to put you away with other childish
    things;

when we long to be loved and accepted
    but feel forever outsiders, excluded from your embrace;

when we envy those who take for granted your close
presence in their lives
    while we feel nothing.

when in bereavement we crave the certainty of eternal life
    but are afraid it is simply wishful thinking.

Risen Lord, as you came to Thomas in his doubts,
offering him your cross-torn body,
come to us, we pray.
Reveal yourself afresh, that we too may say with Thomas:
'My Lord and my God!'

Meriel Chippendale
England

Break Into Our Lives

The two disciples on the Emmaus Road were full of the events of the previous few days, full of their hopes and dreams – and disappointments; full, even of the rumour of a living Christ. And yet – they did not wait to see what was happening in Jerusalem, they did not recognise Jesus as he walked beside them.

How often are we so preoccupied by our own agendas that we, too, fail to see Jesus?

Risen Lord: **break into our lives and help us to see you afresh.**

When we are totally immersed in doing your work,
remind us to spend time with you.

Risen Lord: **break into our lives and help us to see you afresh.**

When we stock our shelves with other people's prayers,
surprise us and meet us in the very core of our being.

Risen Lord: **break into our lives and help us to see you afresh.**

When 'church' means meetings, money and plans for
    restoration,
reveal afresh the living community of those who love you.

Risen Lord: **break into our lives and help us to see you afresh.**

When we label people as 'problems'.
help us to see the unique individuals you love.

Risen Lord: **break into our lives and help us to see you afresh.**

When we assume all those around us to be indifferent or
hostile to you,
convince us once again with your good news and empower us
to pass it on.

Risen Lord: **break into our lives and help us to see you afresh.**

Risen Lord, break into our lives
Help us to look again into the faces of those around us
And to see you afresh.

Meriel Chippendale
England

Index of Authors

271

Index of Titles

273

Monday to Wednesday of Holy Week
On a Roller Coaster

Maundy Thursday
Broken Bread ... Broken Body

Good Friday
The Most Harrowing Time

Holy Saturday
The Waiting Time

Easter Day
The Amazing, Joyful Experience

Eastertide
After the Time of Doubt . . . the Time of Knowing

Acknowledgements and Sources

Every effort has been made to trace copyright ownership; the publisher would be grateful to know of any omissions.

Shrove Tuesday, Ash Wednesday and the Beginning of Lent
A Time for Reflection

Ash Cross, The © Pax Christi, Britain

Ash Wednesday Litany © Pax Christi, Britain

Ash Wednesday Liturgy © Philip Freier

Ash Wednesday Liturgy – A Lenten Witness for Peace © John Ansell and Pax Christi, Britain

Friday After Ash Wednesday, Fr Joseph G. Donders, from *Of Things New* © CAFOD

Not Only in Lent, Lord © Cecily Taylor

Reflection for Ash Wednesday, A, Fr Joseph G. Donders, from *Of Things New* © CAFOD

Sackcloth and Ashes, John Ll Humphreys, from *Kneelers, Prayer Handbook 2001–2002* © United Reformed Church 2001

Saturday After Ash Wednesday, Fr Joseph G. Donders, from *Of Things New* © CAFOD

Shrove Tuesday © Sarah Ingle

Thursday After Ash Wednesday, Fr Joseph G. Donders, from *Of Things New* © CAFOD

True Saying, A, Source unknown

Lent and Passiontide
Into the Wilderness

Calling for a Change of Attitude, Pope John Paul II, from *Food and Land* © CAFOD

Common Welfare, Feliciano Martinez, from *Food and Land* © CAFOD

Compassionate God © Annabel Shilson-Thomas

Conflict © Annabel Shilson-Thomas

Desert © Wendy White

Desert Flowers © Pat Marsh

Desolation © Yorkshire Synod, United Reformed Church

Don't Call Me a Stranger: The Cry of a Migrant © National Council of Churches, India

First Sunday of Lent © Frank Regan

God of All Humanity © Linda Jones/CAFOD

God of the Unknown © Jan Berry, from *Gateways of Grace, Prayer Handbook 1998–99*, United Reformed Church

Hope and Solidarity © Annabel Shilson-Thomas

Hymn for Lent, A © Wendy Ross-Barker

I Believe . . . (1) Prayer of an Ayacucho Youth Group, Comision Episcopal de Accion Social, Lima, Peru, from *Continent of Hope* © CAFOD

I Believe . . . (2), A Peasant Woman, El Salvador, from *Continent of Hope* © CAFOD

I Believe . . . (3), Source unknown, World Council of Churches, from *They Shall Not Rob Us of Hope* © CAFOD

It is Better . . . © Christian Aid, from *They Shall Not Rob Us of Hope*, CAFOD

Litany for Forgiveness, A © W. L. Wallace

Living Water © Yorkshire Synod, United Reformed Church

Love Means Deeds, Javier Torres, from *Continent of Hope* ©
CAFOD

'Man Shall Not Live by Bread Alone' © Heather Johnston

Meditation and Prayers for Lent © Heather Johnston

Money Rules Life, Fr George Anastacio, from *Food and Land* ©
CAFOD

Mothering Sunday © Pat Livingstone

My Prayer is that I will Never Become Indifferent © Ellen
Teague

My Vicar at Work © Y. Mochyn Daear

Pilgrim God © Annabel Shilson-Thomas

Pray for People © Beulah Shakir

Prayer of Confession, A © Elizabeth Welch

Prayer of Dedication, A © Christian Aid

Prayers of Intercession – Conflict © Annabel Shilson-Thomas

Prayers of Intercession – Refugees © Annabel Shilson-Thomas

Refugees © Annabel Shilson-Thomas

Rise Up and Cry Freedom © Annabel Shilson-Thomas

Second Sunday of Lent © Frank Regan

Sending-Out, A © Elizabeth Welch

Serenade to God © Gerald O'Mahony

Something for Lent © Ellen Teague

Temptation to Make Judgements, The © Nigel Pounde,
Church of Scotland

Passiontide
Dying We Live

Palm Sunday
In Triumph and Sorrow

Hope and Solidarity © Annabel Shilson-Thomas

Litany of Triumph and Sorrow, A © Jan Berry, from *Gateways of Grace, Prayer Handbook 1998–99*, United Reformed Church

Palm Sunday © Frank Regan SSC

Song of the Palms © Heather Johnston

Star Cross © Laurentia Johns OSB, Stanbrook Abbey, England

Twenty Centuries Past, John Young, from *Kneelers, Prayer Handbook 2001–2002* © United Reformed Church 2001

Upon A Donkey's Back © Colin Ferguson

Very Special Occasion, A © Peter Grimshaw

Violence © Pat Livingstone

We Pray for the Modern City of Jerusalem © Pat Livingstone

Monday to Wednesday of Holy Week
On a Roller Coaster

Betrayed! © Stephen Brown, from *Gateways of Grace, Prayer Handbook 1998–99*, United Reformed Church

Caleb – Temple Trader © Marjorie Dobson

Cleansing the Temple © Rosemary S. Watts

Daniel – Money-changer © Marjorie Dobson

Dying and Rising, John Ll Humphries, from *Kneelers, Prayer Handbook 2001–2002* © United Reformed Church 2001

Eliazar – the Priest © Marjorie Dobson

Gaius – the Gentile © Marjorie Dobson

God of Hope © Linda Jones/CAFOD

Holy Week © Stephen Brown, from *Gateways of Grace, Prayer Handbook 1998–99*, United Reformed Church

Jesus the Carpenter © Marjorie Dobson

Love Unknown © Marjorie Dobson

Peter © Marjorie Dobson

Spirited Dancer, a Pantomime Figure, Andrew Pratt © Stainer and Bell

Surprising Fragrance, A © Stephen Brown, from *Gateways of Grace, Prayer Handbook 1998–99*, United Reformed Church

Temple Scene © Brian Hudson

Turning the Tables © Marjorie Dobson

Washing One's Hands, Paulo Freire, from *Continent of Hope* © CAFOD

Maundy Thursday
Broken Bread . . . Broken Body

Critic © Marjorie Dobson

Deliver Us and Give Us Peace © John Davies, from *The Crisis of the Cross*, The Canterbury Press

Easter Sonnet, An: Paschal Lamb © Heather Johnston

Eat of the Christ Bread © Colin Ferguson

Guilty, or Not Guilty? © Marjorie Dobson

Heroic Prayer, A © Gerald O'Mahony SJ

I Heard of a Child . . . © Gerald O'Mahony SJ

Jesus in the Garden Weeping, Marjorie Dobson © Stainer and Bell

Jesus Took Off His Robe © Chris Chivers

Let's Go to the Maize Field, Source unknown, from *Continent of Hope* © CAFOD

Maundy Thursday © Sarah Ingle

Neighbour © Marjorie Dobson

Not Us! © Marjorie Dobson

Pilate © Marjorie Dobson

Sharing the Meal © Cecily Taylor

There in a Garden © Colin Ferguson

Truth and Subversion © John Davies, from *The Crisis of the Cross*, The Canterbury Press

Wash Hands – Be Clean? © Edgar Ruddock

Watershed, The © Stephen Brown, from *Gateways of Grace, Prayer Handbook 1998–99*, United Reformed Church

When Jesus Shared © Colin Ferguson

Woman Walked to the Altar, A © Andrew Prasad, Council for World Mission, from *Gateways of Grace, Prayer Handbook 1998–99*, United Reformed Church

You Know Me, Lord © Heather Johnston

Good Friday
The Most Harrowing Time

Blessing the Thorn in the Flesh © Norm S. D. Esdon

Carry this Cross © Heather Johnston

Centurion and the Soldier, The: 'Am I Forgiven?' © Heather Johnston

Condemned Christ, Janet Lees, from *Kneelers, Prayer Handbook 2001–2002* © United Reformed Church 2001

Cross Makers, Ed Cox, from *Kneelers, Prayer Handbook 2001–2002* © United Reformed Church 2001

Crown of Thorns © Pat Marsh

Dying with Dignity © Geoffrey Duncan

Easter People, Jean Sherriff, from *Journey to the Millennium and Beyond* © National Board of Catholic Women

For Three Hours © Pat Marsh

Gift of a Cross © Pat Marsh

Good Friday © Heather Johnston

Good Friday Blessing, A © Norm S. D. Esdon

Good Friday Prayers © Sarah Ingle

Jesus Dies on the Cross © Anthea Dove, from *The Way of the Cross*, Pax Christi/CAFOD

Light © Harry Wiggett

Lord, by Your Cross and Resurrection © Brentwood Diocesan Commission for Justice and Peace

Meditation for Good Friday, A © Heather Pencavel

Modern Calvaries © Doreen Gazey

Myrrh – A Reflection, Anne Hine RSCJ, from *Journey to the Millennium and Beyond* © National Board of Catholic Women

Nightmare © Colin Ferguson, from *Gateways of Grace, Prayer Handbook 1998–99*, United Reformed Church

O Sorrowful Women © Rosemary S. Watts

On the Hillside She Stands Weeping © Pat Livingstone. *Contemporary music for this song is available from the composer, please contact SCM-Canterbury Press.*

Prayer for Good Friday, A © Marjorie Dobson

Prayers for Good Friday © Heather Pencavel

Repentant Thief, The © Anthea Dove

Sacrifice © Marjorie Dobson

Holy Saturday
The Waiting Time

Easter Day
The Amazing, Joyful Experience

Alleluias Echoed, Andrew Pratt © Stainer and Bell

Being Dead Already © Cecily Taylor

Do Not Be Afraid © Duncan Tuck, from *Gateways of Grace, Prayer Handbook 1998–99*, United Reformed Church

Easter Gardens © Y. Mochyn Daear

Easter Morning © Heather Johnston

Easter Sunday © Heather Johnston

First Easter, The – I was There (1) © Heather Johnston

I Was There (2) – Women Who Were There, The © Heather Johnston

Follow in Humility © Raymond Chapman

God's New Life for the Whole World © Heather Pencavel

He Has Won the Peace © Gerard W. Hughes, from *Show Me Your Face*, Pax Christi

Hope, Mary Brogan, from *Journey to the Millennium and Beyond* © National Board of Catholic Women

I Have Seen the Lord © Raymond Chapman

In Christ's Rising from the Dead © W. L. Wallace

It is the Lord © Brentwood Diocesan Commission for Justice and Peace

Love of Jesus, Fill Me © Angela Ashwin from *Woven into Prayer*

Mary in the Garden © Doreen Gazey

Mary Magdalene's Story © Heather Johnston

Mary's Courage, John Ll Humphreys, from *Kneelers, Prayer Handbook 2001–2002* © United Reformed Church 2001

Power of Your New Life, The © Paul Iles from *Waking with Praise*

Resucito © Pat Marsh

Risen Christ © Geoffrey Duncan

Roll Back the Stone © Jill Jenkins

Rose, The © Harry Wiggett

Running to Tell the Good News, Susy Brouard, from *Journeying to the Millennium and Beyond* © National Board of Catholic Women

Sharpened Chill, The, The Flower Strewn Tomb, Andrew Pratt © Stainer and Bell

Tree in Galilee, A © Cecily Taylor

We Are an Easter People © W. L. Wallace

Eastertide
After the Time of Doubt . . . the Time of Knowing

Along the Way © Cecily Taylor

Believing © Y. Mochyn Daear

Blessing in the Resurrection Season, A © Vaughan Jones

Break Into Our Lives, Meriel Chippendale, from *Kneelers, Prayer Handbook 2001–2002* © United Reformed Church 2001

Cock Crowed Twice, The © Penny Bird

Encounter with Us Now Enlivening God © Jill Jenkins

God of Love © Cecily Taylor

Jesus Appears to His Mother After His Death © Susy Brouard

Mary's Remembering, Elizabeth Bradley, from *Journeying to the Millennium and Beyond* © National Board of Catholic Women